AL-GHAZZALI
HIS PSYCHOLOGY OF
THE GREATER STRUGGLE

LALEH BAKHTIAR

ABC International Group, Inc.

Library of Congress Cataloging-in-Publication Data

Laleh Bakhtiar

Al-Ghazzali the Psychology of the Greater Struggle
1. Islamic psychology. 2. Sufism. I. Title.

ISBN: 1-57644-694-9 pbk

Cover design by Rodd Farhadi

Published by
ABC International Group, Inc.
Distributed by
KAZI Publications, Inc.
3023 W. Belmont Avenue
Chicago IL 60618
Tel: 773-267-7001; FAX: 773-267-7002
email: info@kazi.org /www.kazi.org

CONTENTS

INTRODUCTION

". . . be not like those who forgot God and [eventually] God caused them to forget their 'self' . . . " (Q. 59:18-19)

There is nothing more timely today than a translation of the remarkable work on Islam of al-Ghazzali for two reasons. First of all, the results of recent studies of medicine-psychology and religious belief[1] confirm that the religious model works in the healing process so traditional wisdom must be made available in English for all researchers as well as readers to be able to access it and draw upon it for areas of further research. Secondly, at a time when the world is confused by the varying beliefs of Muslims and are interested in studying what the majority of the world's Muslims believe, the works of al-Ghazzali provide the perfect opportunity.

Abu Hamid Muhammad al-Ghazzali was born in the city of Tus, northwestern Iran, in AD 1058.[2] He studied in Tus until he was twenty-seven when he moved to Baghdad. He was appointed as a professor at the Nizamiyyah college there when he was thirty-three. After four years of a strenuous schedule, he underwent a spiritual experience which convinced him that all of the knowledge he had gained was useless in comparison to gnosis or experiential knowledge of the Divine Presence. He realized unless he left his position and was free to search for this knowledge deeper within himself without worldly distractions, he would never attain it. He therefore provided for his family and left for Damascus and other well known cities at that time.

When he was forty-eight he returned to his birthplace where he lived for the next five years until his early death at the age of fifty-three.[3] He left behind over 400 works among them being his famous *Revival of the Religious Sciences (Ihya ulum al-din)* which he wrote in Arabic. Over 2300 pages, it is a compendium of Islamic practices. A few years after he finished the *Revival*, he felt the need to write the same sort of compendium on being a Muslim in Persian. This is the entire work here translated into English for the first time which al-Ghazzali called the *Alchemy of Happiness*. It is a masterful textbook on traditional psychology.[4]

While modern Western psychology focuses on describing emotions, behavior or cognition, that is, what we feel, do and think without recourse to the basic principles or causes, traditional psychology is based on the same three centers, but like all traditional sciences, includes much more. As a result of including metaphysics, theology, cosmology and the natural sciences as the basis or underlying principles for what we feel, do or think, it becomes a wholistic psychology. The goal of traditional psychology is to assume the noble character traits, to overcome our ego which competes for our attention with our God-given instinct to attend to the One God. In this view, there cannot be two wills and therefore our free will has to be disciplined to submit to God's will *(islam)*.

The word psychology comes from the Greek words "psyche" or "soul" and "logos." Psyche also means breath, spirit and refers to the animating principle of the universe. Logos means "word" and in the traditional view it refers to "the Word of God." The science of psychology, then, when it is true to its name, is the study of the Word of God within the human soul or spirit.

Al-Ghazzali's psychology is essentially that of monotheism and unity, the world view that "there is no god, but God" or "there is no deity, but God." It is to see the universe and all that is in it as aspects of the One God. The world view of monotheism (*tawhid*) forms the underlying basis for traditional psychology.

By the word "tradition" we mean *al-din* which has been defined as: "truths or principles of a Divine Origin revealed or unveiled to mankind through a messenger along with the ramifications and application of these principles in different realms including law, social structure, art, symbols, the sciences and embracing Supreme Knowledge along with the means for its attainment."[5]

Tradition (*al-din*) is a point which is at one and the same time the Center and Origin of our being. Traditional psychology is oriented towards helping the individual as well as the human community find that Center as we prepare for the return to our Origin.

A monotheist (*hanif*) like al-Ghazzali regards the whole universe as a unity, as a single form, a single living and conscious thing, possessing will, intelligence, feeling, and purpose, revolving in a just and orderly system in which there is no discrimination no matter what one's gender, color, race, class, or faith be. All comes from God and returns to God, while a multitheist (*mushrik*) views the universe as a discordant assemblage full of disunity, contradiction, and heterogeneity containing many independent and conflicting poles, unconnected desires, customs, purposes, wills, sexes, sects, colors, races, classes, and faiths.

The monotheistic world view sees the universal unity in existence, a unity of three separate relationships: (1) our relationship with others, nature and the universe; (2) our relationship with God; (3) our relationship with our "self." These relationships are not alien to one another; there are no boundaries between them. They move in the same direction. Al-Ghazzali expresses this when he writes:

> Then know that there is a station in gnosis (*marifat*) where, when a person reaches it, he really sees that all that exists is interconnectedness, one with another, and all are like one animate being. The relationship of the parts of the world such as the heavens, the earth, the stars to each other is like the relationship of the parts of one animate being to each other. The relationship of all the world to its Director—from one aspect, not from all aspects—is like the relationship of the kingdom of the body of an animal to the spirit and intellect which are its Director. Until a person recognizes this, that Verily, God created Adam in His image, it cannot be comprehended by his understanding."[6]

Other non-monotheistic religious world views see the Divinity—or even the plural of this—as existing in a special, metaphysical world of the gods, a higher world as contrasted with the lower world of nature and matter. They teach that God is separate from the world, created it and then left it alone. In the monotheistic world view, God has never left and is the destination of the Return. In this view, our "self" fears only one Power and is answerable to only one Judge; turns to one direction (*qiblah*), orienting all hopes and desires to only one Source. A belief in monotheism gives us a sense of independence and liberation from everything other than God and a connectedness to the universe and all that it contains. Submission to God's Will alone liberates us from worshipping anything other than God and rebelling against anything else that purports to be God.

AL-GHAZZALI'S THREE FUNDAMENTALS

Al-Ghazzali sees the basis for traditional psychology leading to self-development—which in esssence is the greater struggle—as consisting of three fundamentals—the same three fundamentals confirmed by modern psychology and scientific studies—affect, behavior and cognition (the ABC of psychology). The first fundamental is knowledge (cognition, awareness or consciousness). The second he calls states (affect or emotion) that that knowledge or awareness produces in us. The third he calls act or deed— the action that results from our emotion that came from our knowledge or awareness of something.

THE FIRST FUNDAMENTAL: KNOWLEDGE (COGNITION)

According to al-Ghazzali, knowledge should be used to come to understand the articles of belief rather than accepting them on faith alone. The articles of belief include: the belief that God is One; the belief that God sent Prophets to guide mankind to Him and that Muhammad (ﷺ) is the Messenger and last Prophet who will be sent (until the end of time when Jesus (عليه السلام) will return) and that the Quran is the last revelation; the belief in angels and the Scriptures; and the belief that after death we will be resurrected in the Hereafter and judged by God who will reward or punish us depending upon our intentions. Al-Ghazzali says: "It is the states of the heart, the place of our intentions, that holds us accountable."[7]

BELIEFS

Our beliefs are the guiding principles that give meaning and direction to our life. They filter our perceptions of the world. When we freely choose to believe something is true, a command is delivered to our spiritual heart (mind) telling us how to represent what we have come to believe to be true. When the process has been accomplished with Divine Grace

(defined by al-Ghazzali as: the harmony, agreement and concord of our will and action with God's will), our beliefs can
become our most effective force for creating the positive and
good in our lives.

In explaining the importance of coming to the realization
of the Oneness of God oneself and not accepting it because
someone has told us, al-Ghazzali says:

> Know that the first duty incumbent upon who-
> ever becomes a Muslim is to know and believe the
> meaning of the utterance "there is no god but God,
> Muhammad is the Messenger of God," which he
> pronounces with his tongue, understands in his
> heart, and believes so that he entertains no doubt
> about it. When he has believed and his heart is
> established firmly upon (that belief)—so that doubt
> cannot touch it—it is sufficient for the basis of being
> (one who submits to God's Will (*muslim*)). Knowing
> it with evidence and proof is an individual duty
> incumbent upon every (one who submits to God's
> Will (*muslim*)). The Prophet (☙) did not command
> the Arabs to seek proofs, to study theology, or to
> look for doubts and replies to those; rather, he was
> content with belief and faith.[8]

He then defines what belief in submission to God's Will
(*islam*) means:

> Know that you have been created and that you
> have a Creator Who is the Creator of all the uni-
> verse and all that it contains. He is One. He has no
> partner nor associate. He is Unique, for He has no
> peer. He always was; His existence has no begin-
> ning. He always shall be; there is no end to His exis-
> tence. His existence in eternity and infinity is a nec-
> essary, for annihilation cannot touch Him. His exis-
> tence is by His own essence. He needs nothing but

nothing is unneedful of Him. Rather, He is established by His Own essence, and everything else is
established through Him.[9]

Al-Ghazzali mentions five sources for our beliefs:

(1) Our environment: how we grow up; models of success
or failure we learn from; what is right and what is wrong;
what is possible and what is impossible.

(2) Our experiences and events as we grow up.

(3) Knowledge: what we know and do not know; that we
continue to educate our "self" from "the cradle to the grave."

(4) Results we have seen achieved in the past, learned
from the stories of past people in the Quran.

(5) Setting new goals to achieve future results.

Future results depend upon how we incorporate our
beliefs—how we view the world—into our own self image.
According to al-Ghazzali, our firm and certain belief in the
Oneness of God should lead us—as it did Prophet Muhammad
(ﷺ)—to the following beliefs:

(i) The belief that everything happens for a reason. We
look for the good and positive in whatever happens.

(ii) The belief that there is no such thing as failure, only
results or outcomes. If we are able to train a falcon to hunt for
us, al-Ghazzali uses as an example, we can train and discipline our rational faculty to control our passions. Al-Ghazzali
says that we should not expect immediate results. Change is
gradual. We need to develop patience, a great virtue in his
view.

(iii) The belief that we must take responsibility for whatever happens. No matter what happens, know and believe
that we are in charge. The Prophet never blamed others for
whatever happened. He never allowed himself to be a victim.
As the Quran says: *"God does not change the condition of a
people until they change what is within themselves."* (Q. 13:11)

(iv) The belief that we need to learn from other people who

are our greatest resource. Treat them with respect and dignity as the Prophet did.

(v) The belief that we need to challenge our profession or line of work and excel in it. Explore new ways of doing things. Increase our sense of curiosity and vitality.

(vi) The belief that there is no success without commitment. Know our outcome in the Hereafter as the Prophet knew. Develop our sensory responses so we know what we are getting and then continue to refine it until we get what we want. Study the key beliefs of the Prophet and then hold tight to them.

In al-Ghazzali's view, if we firmly believe we are among those "who submit to God's Will" (*muslim*), then with our cognition, affect and behavior as understood from the monotheistic point of view as our foundation, we can submit in everything that we say or do. What we believe to be true becomes possible when we know what we want—to be one who submits to God's will—and believe we can achieve it.

STRATEGIES

Developing a strategy is to duplicate our belief system. When we organize the way we think, the way we feel and the way we behave according to our belief system, we have developed a strategy. The ingredients of our strategy are our human experiences. Our experiences are fed from our five outer senses: seeing, smelling, hearing, tasting and touching. Our five senses motivate us to action. When we are aware of what they perceive and keep their perceptions in line with our belief system, we have developed a successful strategy.

The amounts we use of the information provided by our senses is monitored by our spiritual heart (mind). Are the images small or large, bright or unclear, close up or far away?

How we put these together, their order and sequence clarifies our strategy.

With our resource being our "self" consisting of body, spirit, soul and spiritual heart (it is our spiritual heart that centers us), we want to learn what we need to do to organize this resource. How can we have our goal and belief achieve the greatest potential? What is the most effective way to use the resource of our "self" and its subparts? The most effective strategy has always been modeling the behavior of others who have the same goal and the same belief. For the believer, this model is that of the Messenger Muhammad (ﷺ) who was the perfect human being.

Strategies he used included performing the prescribed fast as well as formal prayer, supplication and continuous recitation of the revelation. For the believer, revelation brought both a Law and a Way. Both serve as strategies of how to approach life in the manner in which the model approached life, and knowing that our model did not always do things exactly the same way.

The strategy of Quranic recitation is yet another form of discipline. One of the verses of the Quran: *"Remember Me and I will remember you,"* (Q. 2:152) makes this form of supplication a very rich traditional strategy to attain spiritual energy.

THE SECOND FUNDAMENTAL: STATES
(AFFECT, EMOTION)

Our belief establishes states (emotions, affect) which then result in our actions. In this relationship and all others, our state of mind is important because that determines our emotion and our emotion determines how many resources are available to us. Our emotions depend upon how we feel physically—our breathing, posture, etc.— and how we represent the world to ourselves internally. When we have cleared our spiritual heart of hypocrisy in our acts of worship, our actions are to worship God and we are at the beginning stages of the greater struggle according to al-Ghazzali.

States (affect, emotion) are held or transformed in terms of psychology through moral values that energize us. Our behavior is the result of the state we are in at the time. Our emotional state governors our behavior. Behavior is the result of how we represent the information from our senses internally as well as our muscular tension, posture, physiology.

We have the resources we need to succeed. We have to learn how to access them. We need to learn to take direct control: Once we learn to manage our states (emotions), according to al-Ghazzali, we can modify our behavior. There is a difference of how people react to the same state. The difference depends on their model.

One of the best methods which al-Ghazzali uses over and over again in the *Alchemy* is that of what is today called reframing: changing the way we evaluate what something means. If our culture teaches us that change is a failure of opportunity for learning, we need to become resourceful, to realize that nothing has power over us but the power we give it by our own conscious thoughts. The meaning of any experience depends on the frame we put around it. If we change the context or reference point, the process changes.

We can reframe by context reframing or content reframing. With context reframing, we take a bad experience and show it in another way. With content reframing, we drastically change how we see, hear, or represent a situation. We learn to change the way we represent a situation so we feel differently about it. Now we are at the level of choice instead of reaction. By learning to reframe, we change our emotions so that they empower us. We can either associate or disassociate. If we associate consciously, we learn to change the way we represent things, thereby changing our behavior. We have to aim for congruence between our spiritual heart (mind) and body.

CLARITY OF MORAL VALUES

Clarity of values gives us a sense of who we are and why we do what we do. If we have an internal conflict between our values and our strategy, we will not succeed. Values determine what really matters in life. They provide us with a basis from which to make sound judgments about what makes life worth living.

Al-Ghazzali refers to verses 23:1-10 of the Quran as an example of believers who have succeeded by incorporating Quranic values:

> Certainly will the believers have succeeded: They who during their prayer humbly submissive; those who turn away from ill speech; they who are observant of the poor-due; they who guard their private parts except from their wives and those their right hands possess for indeed, they will not be blamed, but whatever seeks beyond that, then they are the transgressors; and they who are to their trusts and their promises attentive; and they who carefully maintain their prayers. Those are the inheritors. (Q. 23:1-10)

Al-Ghazzali then summarizes the verses to describe a person of good character.

> A person of good character is he who is modest, says little, causes little trouble, speaks the truth, seeks the good, worships much, has few faults, meddles little, desires the good for all, and does good works for all. He is compassionate, dignified, measured, patient, content, grateful, sympathetic, friendly, abstinent, and not greedy. He does not use foul language, nor does he exhibit haste, nor does he harbor hatred in his heart. He is not envious. He is candid, well-spoken, and his friendship and

enmity, his anger and his pleasure are for the sake
of God Most High and nothing more.[10]

In the *Alchemy* (as well as in the *Revival*), al-Ghazzali
devotes the major part of the work to clarity of moral values
by describing in great detail what he calls the Destroyers and
the Deliverers. He not only describes them in each of those
parts, but offers treatment as to how to get rid of them (the
Destroyers) or how to incorporate them into our personality
(the Deliverers). Doing this clarifies the moral values of the
one who submits to God's Will.

As a result of the performance of the acts of worship, if
accompanied by Divine Grace, the one who submits to the Will
of God will be receptive to the adoption of positive dispositions
(the Deliverers) like temperance, courage, wisdom, and justice
and be able to avoid negative dispositions (the Destroyers) like
anger, fear of other than God, cowardice, lust, envy, apathy,
preconsciousness (knowing that you do not know), unconsciousness (not knowing that you do not know) and overcon-
sciousness (knowing but deceiving the self about it), but only
on the condition that others benefit from the positive dispositions one has attained. This, then, makes it encumbent on the
one who has submitted to the Will of God to come to know and
act upon the commands that underlie the relationship of self
to others.

ENERGY

The entire human organism is a complete system that
makes use of energy transformed from food and air to satisfy
its various natural dispositions. Perception (external and
internal senses) and motivation develop, according to traditional psychology, from the animal soul. Motivation is the seat
of impulses towards inclinations which are imprinted on the
external or internal senses and then, through filtering into

what is called the practical intellect (the mind), a response is given. Three energy sources are active in this perspective: natural (venial, *tabiiya*), vital (arterial, *nafsaniyah*), and nervous (*hawaniyah*). These transformed energies are distributed throughout the body. The heart is considered to be the point of contact between the energy of the body and that of the self.

Without the necessary energy, which according to al-Ghazzali comes from spiritual practices, we reach a state of hoplessness and despair. For instance, if someone asked: "If one has been condemned to hardship, what is the benefit of the greater struggle?" Al-Ghazzali explains this attitude:

> Your question is valid. These words are correct in that they are the cause of the illness of our heart. That is, when a sign of a concept that a person has been condemned to hardship falls upon his heart, they cause him to make no effort, neither sowing nor reaping. Such a sign would be when a person who has been condemned to death becomes hungry the thought occurs in his heart not to eat. He says: "What good is bread to me?" He does not extend his hand to eat and he does not eat until by necessity he dies. If he has been condemned to poverty, he says: "Of what use is sowing seed?" so he neither sows nor reaps. And he for whom happiness has been decreed, he has been made aware that wealth and life have been decreed for him. They have been decreed because he has cultivated, done business, and consumed. Therefore, this decree is not invalid; rather it has reasons"[11]

THE THIRD FUNDAMENTAL: ACTIONS
(BEHAVIOR)

Knowledge alone is not sufficient for we who accepted the trusteeship of nature and were endowed with the Divine Spirit which includes our abilities to choose, to discern, and to gain consciousness of our "self." It is through actions based on knowledge that the centered self benefits another as proof of being centered. The major pillars include ritual purity (*taharah*) and ritual prayer (*salah*), ritual fast (*saum*), the paying of the alms tax (*zakah*), the pilgrimage (*hajj*), counseling to positive dispositions and preventing the development of negative ones (*amr bil maruf wa nahy an al-munkar*) and *jihad* or struggle in the Way of God, the greater struggle of which is the inward struggle of the self (*jihad al-akbar*). The last two are the major concern of traditional psychology.

BONDING POWER OR RAPPORT

Bonding and communicating are aspects of action—proof of the extent of transformation through attaining the goal that we had intended. The power to bond with others is an extraordinary human power. It comes in the true sense when bonding develops from the heart and not from either the intellect or the passions. It comes from a deep love for one's fellow human being and arises when we try to meet the needs of others before our own needs, much like a mother with her new born child.

Al-Ghazzali quoting from the Quran, the Prophet and the Companions mentions how important it is to eat with other people and to perform the formal obligatory prayer with other people.

COMMUNICATORS

Believers should conceivably be master communicators on all three levels—with self, with others and with the Source. How we communicate determines the quality of our lives. Through spiritual disciplines like, for example, prescribed fasting, believers are given an opportunity, a challenge. If they are able to communicate that challenge to themselves successfully, they will find the ability to change. This is not to accept prescribed fasting as only a religious duty but rather as a divine challenge, as a chance for growth instead of an experience which limits self. In this way we will become master communicators because our very life will communicate our vision, goal and beliefs to others to help them change for the better, as well.

RELATIONSHIP TO OTHERS

Al-Ghazzali discusses knowledge (cognition), states (affect) and action (behavior) in three relationships: our relationship with others; our relationship with our Creator-Guide; and our relationship with our "self."

The model for this is the *sunnah* of Muhammad (爨) who said, "I was sent to complete the noble qualities of dispositions," explaining that God loves the positive dispositions and not the negative ones. Al-Ghazzali also quotes another Tradition in this regard, "By Him in whose hand is my life, no one shall enter paradise except the one who has positive dispositions." Al-Ghazzali says, "God taught [Muhammad (爨)] all the fine qualities of disposition, praiseworthy paths, reports about the first and last affairs, and matters through which one achieves salvation and reward in future life and happiness and reward in the world to come."

Quoting the Traditions, al-Ghazzali shows the relationship established by the Prophet with others.

> And the Messenger (爨) said: "There are not two persons who love each other for the sake of God that the one most beloved by God is the one loves the other the most." And he (爨) said: "God Most High says: 'My love is a right for those who visit one another for My sake, who love each other for My sake, who are generous to each other with their wealth for My sake, and who aid each other for My sake.'" And he (爨) said: "On the Day of

Resurrection God Most High will say: 'Where are those persons who loved each other for My sake so that I may keep them in My shadow on this day when there is no shade for the people in which to take refuge?'" And he (ﷺ) said: "There are seven persons on the Day of Resurrection who, when there will be no shade for anyone, will be in the shadow of God Most High: the just leader (imam), the young person who began worshipping God Most High at the beginning of his youth, the man who leaves the mosque with his heart attached to the mosque until he returns to it again, two people who love each other for the sake of God Most High and who come together for that and separate for that, the person who remembers God Most High in private and whose eyes fill with tears, and the man who when called by a magnificent and beautiful woman says to her: 'I fear God Most High,' and the man who gives voluntary charity with his right hand so that the left hand has no knowledge of it." And he (ﷺ) said: "No one visits a brother for the sake of God Most High save that an angel cries out, saying: 'Be happy and blessed! Thine is the heaven of God Most High!'"

And he (ﷺ) said: "A man was going to visit a friend. God Most High sent an angel in his path who asked: 'Where are you going?' He replied: 'To visit such-and-such a brother.' (The angel) asked: 'Do you have some business with him?' He said: 'No.' (The angel) asked: 'Are you related to him in some way?' He said: 'No.' (The angel) asked: 'Has he done something good for you?' He answered: 'No.' (The angel) said: 'Then why are you going to him?' He answered: 'I love him for the sake of God.' (The angel) said: 'Then, God Most High has sent me to you to give you the good news that God Most High loves you because of your love for him, and has made heaven an obligation for both of you your-selves.'" And the Messenger (ﷺ) said: "The

strongest resort of faith is love and enmity for the
sake of God Most High."[12]

Al-Ghazzali describes relationships with others ranking
them in degrees.

> The first degree is that you love someone for
> some reason linked with him, but that motive is
> religious and for the sake of God Most High; as you
> like your teacher because he teaches you knowl-
> edge. That friendship is of a divine nature since
> your aim for (acquiring) this knowledge is the
> Hereafter, not rank or wealth. If the object be the
> world, that friendship is not of that kind. If you love
> your student so that he learn from you and may
> obtain the pleasure of God Most High through
> learning, (you) too obtain the spiritual reward of
> teaching. This is for the sake of God Most High. But
> if you love (him) for the sake of dignity and retinue,
> it will not be of that kind. If a person gives volun-
> tary charity and likes a person on the condition that
> he deliver that to the poor; or he invites some poor
> people and likes a person who prepares a good
> meal, then such friendship is for the sake of God.
> Indeed, if one likes someone and gives him bread
> and clothing to give him the leisure to worship
> (God), it is friendship for the sake of God, since his
> motive is the peace of mind for worship.
> Many religious scholars and worshippers have
> had friendships with the rich and powerful for this
> reason. Both were counted as friends for the sake of
> God Most High. Moreover, if one loves his own wife
> because she keeps him from corruption and because
> of the bringing forth of children who will supplicate
> for him, such love is for the sake of God Most High
> and everything you spent for her is a voluntary
> charity. Indeed, if one loves his student for two rea-
> sons: one that he serves him and the other that he

gives him the peace of mind to perform his worship, that part which is for worship is counted as love for the sake of God most High and there is spiritual reward for it.

The second degree is greater. It is that one love a person for the sake of God without having any expectations from him; instead, it is by reason of obedience to God and for the love of Him that he loves the other. Moreover, because he is a servant of God and created by Him—such friendship is divine. It is greater because this arises from the excess of one's love of God Most High, so much so that it reaches the boundaries of passionate love. Whoever is in love with someone, loves (that person's) district and neighborhood. He loves the walls of (that person's) house; indeed, he loves the dog roaming the quarter's streets, and he likes that dog more than other (dogs). He is compelled to love the friend of his beloved, and beloved of his beloved, the people who obey the commands of his beloved; (the beloved's) servants, captives, or relatives; all of these he loves out of necessity, for his love spreads to whatever has a relation with his beloved. As his love increases so it does with the others who follow and are connected with the beloved.[13]

ESTABLISHING THE RELATIONSHIP BETWEEN THE SELF AND OUR CREATOR-GUIDE

This relationship is established, according to al-Ghazzali, through the commands of worship (*ibadah*), which are the most fundamental means of communication between our "self" and God. They embody the same three aspects: knowledge (cognition), states (affect, process) and action (behavior). One who submits to the Will of God seeks knowledge of particular guidance. This produces a "state" (emotion) in the self which then responds with an action as al-Ghazzali explains:

Know that object and kernel of all acts of worship are the remembrance of God Most High; that the buttress of Islam is obligatory formal prayer, the object of which is the remembrance of God Most High. As He said: *Surely (formal) prayer prevents lewdness and evil, and indeed the remembrance of God is greater (than all else).* (Q. 29:45)

Reading the Quran is the most meritorious of the acts of worship, for the reason that it is the word of God Most High: (reading or reciting it) is remembering Him. Everything that is in it all cause a renewal of the remembrance of God, may He be praised and exalted. The object of fasting is the reduction of the carnal appetite so that the heart, liberated from the annoyance of the carnal appetites, becomes purified and the abode of remembrance; for when the heart is filled with carnal appetite, it is not possible to remember (Him); nor does (the remembrance) affect one. The object of the greater pilgrimage, which is a visit to the House of God, is the remembrance of the Lord of that House and the incitement of longing for meeting Him.

Thus the inner mystery and the kernel of all of the acts of worship are remembrance. Indeed, the basis of Islam is the declaration: "there is no god but God"; this is the source of remembrance. All other acts of worship stress this remembrance. God's remembrance of you is the fruit of your remembrance of Him; what fruit could be greater than this? For this He said: *So remember Me, I shall remember you.* (Q. 2:152)

This remembrance must be continuous. If it is not continuous, it should be most of the time; for salvation is tied to it. For this He said: *And remember God much; perhaps you will be successful.* (Q. 62:10) He says that if you have the hope of salvation, the key to that is much remembrance, not a little, and more frequently, not less.

And for this He said: *Those who remember God standing, sitting, and lying down.* (Q. 3:191) He praised these people because they do not neglect (remembrance) standing, sitting, lying down, or in any condition. And He said: *Remember thy Lord, (O Muhammad), within thyself humbly and with awe, in a soft voice, in the morning and in the evening, and be not of the neglectful.* (Q. 7:205) He said: "*Remember Him with weeping, fear, and in conceal-ment, morning and evening, and do not neglect (this) at any time.*"

The Messenger (ﷺ) was asked: "What is the best of acts?" He answered: "That you die with your tongue moist with the remembrance of God Most High." And he said: "Should I not inform you of the best of your actions—the most acceptable to the King, may He be exalted—and your highest degrees, that which is better than giving alms of sil-ver and gold, and better than shedding your blood in battle against enemies in defense of the faith?" They asked: "What is that, O Messenger of God?" He said: "The remembrance of God." The remem-brance of God Most High! And he said: "Whoever remembering me engages in worshipful supplica-tion of God, his gift is, in my opinion, greater and better than giving (charity) to beggars." And he said: "The remembrer of God Most High among the heedless is like a living person amongst the dead, or like a green tree amongst dead vegetation, or like the warrior for the faith who stands fighting amongst those fleeing. . ."[14] In summary, the strength of one's love for God Most High is in accor-dance with the strength of one's faith. The stronger one's faith, the more overwhelming one's love is.[15]

KNOW YOUR "SELF"

The most important relationship for the purposes of tradi-tional psychology is that of our relationship to our "self." Our "self" as we have seen, consists of body, spirit, soul and spiritual heart. We turn now to the *Alchemy*'s Prolegomena (added here by al-Ghazzali, it does not appear in the *Revival*) where al-Ghazzali explores how to come to know the "self" in great detail.

*****

The traditional method of teaching a text is for the teacher to read it part by part with a class of students and then comment on what the text is saying. This is the method used next taking just the first subsection of Topic One of the Prolegomena, "Knowing Yourself" which appears in the following paragraphs in bold. The commentary and explanations that follow are enhanced with other sections of al-Ghazzali's writings in the *Alchemy* which are inset for clarity. If we were sitting in al-Ghazzali's classroom, this is the method he would be using.

COMMENTARY ON TOPIC ONE OF THE PROLEGOMENA: KNOW YOURSELF

1 Know that the key to the knowledge of God, may He be honored and glorified, is knowledge of one's own self. For this it has been said: He who knows him "self" knows his Lord. And it is for this that the Creator Most High said: *We shall show them Our signs on the horizons and within themselves so that it will become evident to them that it is the Truth*. (Q. 41:53) He said: We show them Our signs in the universe and in (their) selves so that the true nature of the Truth may become revealed to them.

Al-Ghazzali begins with the famous Tradition (*hadith*), "He who knows himself, knows his Lord." There is another that could be added: "Words of wisdom (knowledge) are the lost objects of the faithful; he must claim them wherever he finds them." The quest for knowledge is a religious obligation in Islam. Al-Ghazzali quotes another Tradition of the Prophet: Know that the Prophet (ﷺ) spoke thus: 'The quest for knowledge is incumbent upon every Muslim.' Seeking knowledge is a religious duty incumbent upon all Muslims.[1]

Al-Ghazzali continues to show that knowledge differs depending upon one's intentions.

> But all of the scholars have disputed (about this): "What knowledge is this (to which the Prophet referred)?" The scholastic theologians say that it is the science of scholastic theology by which the gnosis (*marifat*) of God Most High is obtained. The religious jurisprudents say that it is the knowledge of religious jurisprudence by which the lawful and unlawful are distinguished. The Traditionists say that is the study of the Traditions and the prac-

tice (of the Prophet) which are the sources of the
religious studies. The mystics say that is the knowledge of the states of the heart, for the way of the
servant (of God) to God is through his heart.

Each of these groups exalts its own knowledge.
Our view is that one particular knowledge is not
meant (by the Prophet's words) and that neither are
all of these studies needed. . . . [2]

Gnosis is defined as being continuously in the Divine
Presence or sacred knowledge by al-Ghazzali:

So, from all of this it has become known that
learning is a religious duty imposed upon all
Muslims. Every Muslim stands in need of some
kind of knowledge; but such knowledge is not of one
kind. The obligations upon a person vary. Indeed,
they change with conditions and times. However,
there is no one without some kind of a need for
knowledge. It is for this that the Prophet (ﷺ) said:
'There is no Muslim for whom the seeking of knowledge is not a religious duty." That is, the search for
the knowledge which he needs in his tasks.[3]

In regard to knowledge of the states of the heart al-
Ghazzali views this as the highest form of knowledge. A know-
er (gnostic, mystic) seeks: ". . . knowledge known as gnosis."
Gnosis, *marifat, irfan*, a word we will meet often throughout
al-Ghazzali's *Alchemy of Happiness* is knowledge of God that
is actually experienced by the seeker. How does one obtain it?
Al-Ghazzali states it succinctly: "The beginning of all
gnoses (*marifat-ha*) is that one come to know oneself and God
Most High." And then he explains gnosis in more detail:

Know that the first station of the stations of
religion is certainty and gnosis (*marifat*). Then, fear
arises from gnosis; and from fear asceticism,

patience, and repentance arise. Truth, sincerity and care in the remembrance (of God) and continuous meditation appear from fear and from them familiarity and love arise, and this is the end of the stations. Satisfaction, commitment, and zeal: all of these follow upon love. As a consequence, the alchemy of (spiritual) happiness, after certainty and gnosis, is fear; whatever is after that cannot be managed without it. . . .[4]

And know that the divisions of the kinds of gnosis (*maarif*) of faith are many:

The first is sanctification, that you know that God, may He be honored and exalted, is pure and free of all attributes of created things and all that comes to thought and imagination. The expression of this is: "Glory be to God" (*subhan al-Lah*)! (ii) The second is that you know that He is in this purity unique and He has no partner. The expression of this is: "There is no but God" (*la ilaha illa-l-Lah*)! (iii) The third is that you know that everything that exists, all of it, is from Him and is His blessing. The expression of this condition is: "Praise be to God" (*al-hamdu lil-Lah*)! This is beyond both of the other two because both kinds of those kinds of gnosis appear beneath it. It was for this that the Messenger (ﷺ) said: "'Glory be to God!' is ten good deeds, 'There is no god but God!' is twenty good deeds, and 'Praise be to God!' is thirty good deeds." Those good deeds are not the movements of the tongue with those words; rather, those good deeds are the gnoses appearing in the heart which those words express. This is the meaning of the knowledge of gratitude.

As for the state of gratitude, it is the joy which appears in the heart from this gnosis (*marifat*); for everyone who sees a blessing from someone rejoices in that.[5]

Included in the knowledge that we need for traditional

psychology is knowledge of Divine Grace (the harmony, agree-ment, or concord of our will and action with God's Will)[6] and Guidance. As an exponent of traditional psychology—which has its basis in metaphysics—al-Ghazzali emphasizes the need to seek Divine Grace and Guidance in undertaking the greater struggle. It is his view that Divine Grace is always present whether we seek it or not but consciously seeking it increases the chances of success in this world and the next.[6]

As al-Ghazzali points out, Divine Guidance—which oper-ates through "nature in its mode of operation" or process—has established Signs between the Creator and our "self" as a means of communication. *We (God the Creator) shall show them (human beings) Our Signs upon the horizon (universe) and within themselves (the self) until it is clear to them (human beings) that He (God) is the Real (haqq)."* (41:53) When we become conscious of our "self" and then freely choose to learn to read and to live by the Signs without and within, we will have submitted to God's Will (*islam*). We will have completed the process of perfecting nature's process or "mode of operation" within us. We will become centered and bal-anced, exhibiting the noble character traits, having gained experiential knowledge (*gnosis*) of the oneness of God (monotheism, *tawhid*) reflected in nature and within our "self."

Signs of God in nature—which includes all of the universe from the largest galaxy of stars and the planets to the small-est living organism on earth—are both external to us and internal. The study of the external Signs forms the subject of the various Natural Sciences the human being has developed to "understand" the Divine Creation like cosmology, astrono-my, philosophy, biology, chemistry, and so forth as well as the science of revelation, gaining knowledge about the Quran where the 6000 some verses are each called a Sign (*ayah*).

The study of internal Signs is part of what is called practical philosophy (*hikmat-i amali*) and includes the sciences of ethics, economics (including home economics) and politics. What was known as the study of ethics is today called traditional psychology. The goal of traditional psychology—to develop noble character traits—is to become a moral and ethical person by disciplining our free will in a process called "the greater struggle" (*jihad al-akbar*). Traditional psychology for al-Ghazzali (and all traditionalists) begins by referring to the "place" of the human being in the universe.

THE COVENANT BETWEEN SELF AND GOD

As the last creation of nature's Creator, we human beings occupy a special place in nature because out of all of nature it is only within us that God breathes His Spirit. It is this infusion of the Divine Spirit which allows us to become conscious of "self," an advantage no other aspect of nature has. Therefore, even though all of nature, the universe, and the cosmos are divinely created, only we have "consciousness of self."

In the traditional perspective this gift of consciousness was granted to our human spirit when we accepted the trust of the heavens and the earth. The Quran says: "*We offered the trust to the heavens and the earth and the mountains, but they refused to carry it and were afraid of it, and the human being carried it.*" (33:72) The acceptance of the trust includes the covenant with the Lord (Rabb) as the Quran says, "*And when your Lord took the seed of the children of Adam from their loins,*" and [asked], "*Am I not your Lord?*" and they bore witness, "*Yea, we do bear witness . . .*" so that they not respond on the Day of Judgment by saying, "*We were unaware of this.*" (7:172)

Through this covenant, we human beings became the trustee or representative of God on earth and accepted the vice-gerency of the universe. The rules and regulations for this position are spelled out in traditional psychology. We accepted not only the outward trust of nature and the universe, but the inner trust as well—to complete and perfect our human nature. God gives it to us perfect and complete and it is the nurturing process—how we are raised and the environment in which we grow—that takes us away from our innate nature.[7] The goal of traditional psychology to assume noble character traits is so that upon the Return to God—from whence all things came—we will return as the vice-gerent (*khalifa*) of the outer world as well as of our inner "self."

SEEKING DIVINE GRACE

In order to carry out the duties of the trusteeship, Divine Grace is sought. It is always available if sought as the Sign says: *God turns to those who turn to Him*. (Q. 2:160) Al-Ghazzali goes so far as to say that without Divine Grace—which is always present whether invoked or not—there is no conscious communication between the Creator and the trustee. In other words, without consciousness of self, communication of the regulations of the trust remains indirect and preconscious or even, perhaps, unconscious. Al-Ghazzali defines Divine Grace as "the harmony, agreement, or concord of our will and action with God's Will."[8] It appears as a Sign, "*That is the Grace of God, a free gift which He gives to Whom He Wills*," (Q. 5:54)[9] and consists of four stages: guidance from God (*hidayah*), sound judgment (*rushd*), confirmation (*tasdid*), and support (*tayid*). Guidance from God is of two types: universal guidance through nature (*takwini* or *khalq*) and particular guidance through revelation (*tashrii* or *khulq*).

The verse or Sign of the Quran, "*[God] gave unto everything its nature and further gave it guidance*," (Q. 20:50) according to the traditional perspective, indicates God as the Creator and the Guide of all nature.

The first kind of guidance is *takwini* or primordial, uni-

versal guidance which all of nature receives, human or otherwise, as part of their *fitrat* or innate nature or natural disposition. This universal guidance regulates whatever is created
in nature through a natural, unreflective process, to imple-
menting God's Will. Al-Ghazzali expands on this type of guidance by saying, "He guides the young bird to pick up seeds
from the time of its hatching; He guides the bee to build its
house in a hexagonal form . . ."[10]

Our human nature in the traditional perspective holds
within itself all that came before it in creation, not in material terms, but in terms of "nature in its mode of operation,"
which is part of universal guidance. Mineral, plant, animal,
and human "souls" each contribute to a part of the development and perfection of "nature's mode of operation." Minerals
contribute preservation of the forms of the four elements of
earth, air, fire, and water and their properties of cold and dry,
hot and wet, hot and dry, and cold and wet, respectively. The
plant soul contributes the ability to assimilate food, to grow,
and to reproduce and the animal soul contributes perception
and motivation.

At the time of the conception of the human body, it was
completed with what is known as the infusion of the Divine
Spirit (Q. 15:29) *"I breathed into him of My Spirit."* Out of this
union of body and "spirit" or "breath" was born the "soul"
which inclines downwards towards the body and the spiritual
heart which inclines upwards towards the infused spirit or
breath. These four aspects—body, spirit (or breath), soul and
spiritual heart make up the human "self." As the last offspring
of creation, we received the gift of consciousness as part of our
natural disposition, a gift that we share only with the Creator
because of the covenant we made with God and the acceptance
of the trusteeship or vice-gerency. This, then, is the world of
creation guided by universal guidance.

The second type of guidance refers to guidance acquired

through God's commands. The world of command is guided by the particular guidance of revelation. As it is rational in orientation, it is our special guidance alone as human beings. If accepted as guidance in the perspective of "submission to the Will of God" (*islam*), particular guidance becomes yet another gift to one who actually does "submit to the Will of God" (*muslim*). It is a particular kind of guidance, in a sense, because it speaks to human consciousness. It is to elucidate this kind of guidance that God sends Prophets and the Divine Law as reinforcement against the forgetful and negligent human beings declaring on the Day of Judgment, "*We were unaware of this.*" (Q. 7:173)

Guidance acquired through revelation as a stage of Divine Grace or Assistance is considered to be a free gift from God because the giving was not obligatory on His part. However, al-Ghazzali makes an important distinction here. God's communication through revelation, by which we can acquire guidance, helps us know the positive traits of our divinely bestowed natural disposition, but does not compel us to actualize them through our actions or practices. We are free to make the choice to follow the world of command—particular guidance through revelation (*tashrii* or *khulq*)—or not to do so. If we do not choose to be guided by particular guidance that is our choice. However, we will still be guided by universal (*takwini* or *khalq*) guidance just as the rest of nature is. We are compelled by universal guidance while we have free will in regard to choose or not choose particular guidance.

While we do not want to digress from our main point, there may be a need to further explain universal guidance. According to traditional psychology, the human being was born with a body infused with God's spirit. These two, when joined, brought the soul into being. The body was created out of water and earth (cold and wet, cold and dry) while the spirit was created out of air and fire or light (hot and wet, hot and dry). The soul contains all four properties—water, earth, air and fire—and their properties of cold, hot, wet and dry.

These properties or qualities join in various proportions to create the mineral soul which preserves them. Out of that grows the plant soul which gives us the ability to digest and assimilate food, to grow and to reproduce. Out of the mineral and plant souls comes the animal soul which gives us perception and motivation.

All of these abilities —the ability to grow, to reproduce, etc.—belong to the world of creation and fall under universal guidance. They involve involuntary processes which do not require consciousness to function. They are natural processes.

However, as human beings who have consciousness, if we rely solely on universal guidance, we will not succeed in "submitting to the Will of God" (*islam*) and completing the perfection of nature in its mode of operation because without particular guidance, there is the possibility that we will not be able to sufficiently strengthen our free will to oppose the satanic forces (ego) within us. Divine Grace as Guidance from God, strengthens our will power so that we gain greater conformity to God's Will. Without Divine Grace we make choices whereby our mineral, plant, and animal nature are strengthened as opposed to our free will being guided to follow the advice of reason. In other words, without the guidance of the Prophets and the Divine Law—which are part of revelation—we will live by universal guidance alone, possibly never achieving our full potential and possibly never completing the perfection of nature in its mode of operation which God so Willed when He infused His Spirit into us.

Particular guidance (*tashrii, khulq*) enhances our natural disposition of conscience and our power of discernment to know the difference between good and bad, right and wrong, or positive virtues and negative vices. It also helps us regulate the states of our "self" at every level of change and transformation towards completing the perfection of nature's process at its highest level. Al-Ghazzali refers to the Signs, *"But to those who follow (tashrii) guidance, He increases their guidance and bestows on them piety."* (Q. 47:17) *Say: God's guidance is the guidance* (Q. 6:71) *Whenever God wills to guide a human being, He enlarges his breast for surrender (to Him) (islam).* (Q. 6:125)

In addition to Guidance from God in both its universal and particular forms, Divine Grace contains three other previously eluded to stages—sound judgment, confirmation and support—to all people in proportion to their seeking Divine Grace. The Sign, *"And We verily gave Abraham of old sound judgment and were aware of him,"* (Q. 21:51) confirms the second stage of Divine Grace—sound judgment—which is present when we sense God is aware of us. The Sign that we have received confirmation of Divine Grace is when we are aware that our will and what we intend have resulted in an action that is directed to God. This is the third stage referred to by al-Ghazzali as confirmation *(tasdid)*. The final stage of Divine Grace is support *(tayid)* which is referred to by the Sign, *". . . when I supported you with the Spirit."* (5:110) The Sign that we have received support of Divine Grace is when we become aware that we have developed greater insight.

Al-Ghazzali elaborates on Divine Grace:

> There is no blessing without the Divine Grace of Divine Guidance. The meaning of Divine Grace is the setting up of a concordance between the decree of God Most High and the will of the servant of God. It is both in evil and in good. However, the term has customarily come to refer to the joining of the desire of the servant of God and the (Divine) Decree in which lies the servant's well-being. This is fulfilled with four things:
> (1) The first is guidance of which no one is not

in need, because if a person is seeking the happiness of the Hereafter and if he does not know the way but knows the wrong way, what is the benefit? Therefore, the creation of things without guidance is not enough. For this, God Most High put (us) under an obligation for both, saying: [(Moses) said: *Our Lord]* is He Who gave unto everything its nature, then guided it aright; (Q. 20:50) and He said: *(God) is He Who measures then guides.* (Q. 87:3) And know that there are three degrees of guidance:

(i) The first (degree) (guidance) is that one distinguish between good and evil. He has given this to all rational beings: some (distinctions are made) by the faculty of reason and some by the words of the prophets. By that which He said: *And guide him to the parting of the two ways?* (i.e. good and evil) (Q. 90:10) He desired to show the way of good and evil to (the Messenger). By that which He said: *(The Thamud) preferred blindness to guidance,* (Q. 41:17) He meant that whoever is deprived of this guidance, either by reason of envy or pride, or because of worldly affairs, does not heed the prophets or the religious scholars; if not, no rational person would not heed. (ii) The second degree (sound judgment) is the special guidance that appears little by little between religious conduct and the greater struggle, and opens the way to the underlying purpose. This is the fruit of the greater struggle. As He said: *As for those who struggle in Us, We surely guide them to Our ways.* (Q. 29:69) He said for those that strive: We Ourself shall guide them to Our ways. He did not say: "We Ourself shall guide (him) *to Us.*" And that which He said is also this: *Those who are guided aright, then He increases in guidance. . .* (Q. 47:17) (iii) The third degree is the guidance reserved for the select. This light appears in the world of prophethood and sainthood. This guidance is to God Most High, not to the way of God. This is in a manner for which the intellect does not have the strength, for it comes of itself to (him). That which He said: *Say: Lo! The guidance of God is the Guidance!* (Q. 6:71) means that it is absolute guidance (par excellence). He called it *"Revival" (ihya)* and said: *Is he who is dead and We have raised him unto life and set for him a light wherein he walks among men as him whose similitude is in utter darkness?* (Q. 6:122)

(2) As for sound judgment, it is that the impulse to travel the way with guidance appear in one. As He said: *And had certainly given Abraham his sound judgment.* (Q. 21:51) A child who has reached puberty does not have sound judgment if he knows how property is preserved and does not do so, even though he has received guidance.

(3) As for finding confirmation of guidance, it is that the motion of his limbs move with ease from the aspect of that which is right so that he quickly attain his goal. So, the fruit of guidance is in gnosis *(marifat)*; the fruit of sound judgment is motive and will; and the fruit of (the confirmation) of guidance is in the power and tools of movement.

(4) As for support of guidance, it is composed of the help of the angels from the unseen internally with the sharpness of perception, and externally with the power of strength and movement. As He said: . . .*when I supported you with the Spirit* (Q. 5:110) Temperance is close to this. That is that an impediment appear inside one blocking the way to sin and the darkness of the way, but one does not fully understand where the impediment comes from. As He said: *And she certainly desired him, and he (Joseph) would have desired her if it had not been that he saw proof of his Lord.* (Q. 12:24)

These are the blessings of the world which are the provision for the Hereafter, and these have need of other causes, and these causes have need of other causes, until at the end (of the sequence) one reach-

> es the Guide of the Perplexed and the Lord of Lords,
> Who is the Causer of Causes. A discussion of all the
> links in the chain of causes would be lengthy: let
> what we have said here suffice."[11]

Based on al-Ghazzali's description, the Guidance we receive through sound judgment, confirmation and support will reflect in our intentions which consist of desire, will power and knowledge. We use our will power to motivate us and make our intentions known to ourself in establishing our relationship with God, with the creation and with our "self." We do this, according to al-Ghazzali, through three stages: knowledge (cognition), states (affect) and acts (behavior).

Our cognition based in the certain belief in the Oneness of God and prophethood of Muhammad (ﷺ) results in our strategies reflecting that belief system. Our affect based in noble character traits exhibited in the Most Beautiful Names that formed the character of Prophet Muhammad (ﷺ) energize our total "self" (body, spirit or breath, soul and spiritual heart). This leads to healing and centering—to the extent of God's Will and our motivation—in the complete and perfect human nature God gave us, holding fast to our covenant and maintaining our trusteeship of nature. Our behavior then becomes habituated to bonding with our Creator, the universe, friends, family and other human beings in such a way that we communicate with them through the most beautiful character by holding our passions—lust and anger—in check by our sense of reason while maintaining our reason to be balanced and centered in fairness and justice. This is how we exhibit our love of God which, according to al-Ghazzali, is the highest state we human beings can attain.

Adding to our various kinds of knowledge, in addition to knowledge about Divine Guidance and Grace, is the knowledge of intention. Al-Ghazzali explains:

> Intention consists of three things: desire, will power and knowledge. Desire for something is what prompts will power and sets it to work. This is also called motivation, purpose or intention. All three mean the same thing.[12]

This is knowledge about how important making our intention known is according to traditional psychology because it is through our intentions that we will be judged in the Hereafter. We should also know as we are trying to get to know our "self" that the best intention we can have is to do whatever we do for God's sake alone as al-Ghazzali points out:

> Now that you have learned that the meaning of intention is motivation to act, know that there is the person who is motivated to acts of devotion because of the fear of hell. There is the person who is motivated by the blessings of Paradise. Whoever acts for the sake of Paradise is the slave of his belly and his genitalia and is killing himself until it comes to the point that he satisfies his belly and his genitalia. And he who acts out of fear of hell is like the bad slave who does not work except out of fear of his master. Both of these have nothing to do with God Most High. On the contrary, the admirable servant of God is he who does what he does for the sake of God Most High, not in the hope of Paradise or in the fear of hell. He is like the person who looks upon his beloved for the sake of the beloved, not because his beloved gives him silver and gold; for whoever looks for the sake of silver and gold, his beloved is silver and gold. Consequently, whoever's beloved and adored one is not the beauty and majesty of the Divine Presence cannot be so motivated.[13]

2 In a word, there is nothing closer to you than you.

If you do not know yourself, how can you know anything else? Indeed, if you say you know your "self," you are in grievous error! You know nothing more about your "self" than your head, face, hands, feet, flesh, and external skin! All you know about your insides is that when you are hungry you must eat; when you anger, you fight; when lust or (sexual) appetite overcomes you, you seek to copulate. In this, you are the equal of the beasts of burden!

Our "self" consist of body, spirit, soul and spiritual heart as has been previously described. When al-Ghazzali refers to soul in the *Alchemy*, he is invariably referring to the animal soul (*nafs al-ammarah*). What is this animal soul and what purpose does it have?

It is important here to know the animal soul in great detail as it is the animal soul that is our enemy in our greater struggle.

The word "soul" can be confusing in traditional psychology because necessary descriptions are often not given in traditional texts so the lines tend to blur particularly between the concepts of soul, spirit and heart. Here we will try to clarify what traditionist mean by soul in general and animal soul in particular.

We have previously referred to the mineral and plant souls as well as the animal soul. In addition the Quran refers to the blaming soul and the soul at peace among others. According to al-Ghazzali only the animal soul when seen within the human being plays a negative role in trying to prevent us from succeeding in the greater struggle. The other aspects—the blaming soul, the soul at peace, etc.—are positive aspects of the soul which are often referred to as the heart and the spirit respectively.

Here we will only be describing the animal soul.

The animal soul or "passions" in the traditional perspective consists of two major systems: affective (lust, appetite, preserve the species, attraction to pleasure) and behavioral (anger, preserve the individual, avoidance of harm/pain). We have met these two concepts previously as states (affect, emotion or A) and acts (behavior or B).

Al-Ghazzali explains the importance of the opposing cold-hot qualities between these two aspects of the animal soul:

> And the reason for anything's not coming into existence in perfection and beauty is that there is some attribute working in opposition to it. It may be that in that opposition there is a purpose for some other work: for it is not possible for fire to accept the coolness and delicacy of water, because heat does not accept cold as it is its opposite. Too, its heat is the point (of its existence); eliminating (that quality) from it would also be a deficiency. In fact, the moisture from which He created the fly He created because the fly is more perfect than that moisture; the moisture is (potentially) capable of that perfection; (realizing that potential) was not held back from it, for such a restriction would be stinting. (The fly) is more perfect because in it are life, power, sensation, movement, and strange shapes and organs which are not in that moisture.*[14]

THE AFFECTIVE SYSTEM

The affective/emotive or "attraction to pleasure" system is the most basic aspect of the animal soul and its function is to preserve the human species. This aspect of the animal soul is referred to as *shahawat* (concupiscence) by al-Ghazzali. It has been translated as carnal desires, lust (appetites) or our bestial qualities. Lust is born of water and earth (cold and wet and cold and dry respectively) and has a downward tendency.

It is that part of our "self" that seeks, desires and is attracted to pleasure.

THE BEHAVIORAL SYSTEM

The second system to be generated as part of the animal soul, is the behavioral or "avoidance of pain" system to preserve us as an individual. Al-Ghazzali refers to this as *ghadhab* (irascible), anger or our predatory qualities. Anger is born of fire and air and has an upward inclination. The behavioral system is considered to be in a preconscious state in the sense that it is capable of learning discipline and modifying itself if regulated by a balanced cognitive system which will be discussed below.

THE AFFECTIVE / EMOTIVE AND BEHAVIORAL SYSTEMS (THE ANIMAL SOUL)

Al-Ghazzali compares the animal soul (affect-behavior) to a stubborn animal and how to discipline it.

> The similitude of this animal soul is the stubborn beast of burden which we satisfy by first withholding its fodder until it is tamed. Another is that we remove the fodder from before it so that it does not see it; another is that we give it that amount which calms it down. Each of these three treatments are the same for the appetite. It is the weakening of the appetite.[15]

Al-Ghazzali gives another example of the animal soul.

> The similitude of anger is that of a hunting dog; the similitude of the carnal appetite or lust is that of a horse; and the similitude of reason is that of a rider. A horse is sometimes refractory and some-

> times obedient and trained. A dog is sometimes
> taught and sometimes it reverts to its own nature.
> Until the one is taught and the other trained, there
> is no hope for the rider's obtaining any game;
> indeed, there is the fear that he will be killed, that
> the dog may attack him, or that the horse may
> throw him to the ground.[16]

The affective-behavioral systems or "the passions" are the irrational systems within our "self." They can corrupt our rational system and seduce our free-will. They work through both our internal sense of imagination and through our impulses to move our "self" to attracting pleasure (lust) or avoiding harm (anger).

Our abilities to be motivated and to perceive arise out of our animal soul. When we desire something that motivates our will power to obtain it. When we desire to escape from a dangerous situation, that desire motivates our will power to flee. So while al-Ghazzali describes states (affect, attraction to pleasure, emotion lust) as separate from acts (behavior, avoidance of pain, anger) as the second and third of his fundamentals of traditional psychology, they are actually one thing—the animal soul. There is a continuous tension between them on the one hand trying to obtain pleasure while on the other trying to avoid harm.

According to traditional psychology the affective or emotional system is programmed to instinctively attract love and pleasure while the behavioral system is programmed to avoid harm and pain. The affective system receives its energies from the organ of the liver through the veins to attract to pleasure. It is the most basic drive of human nature. The behavioral system, on the other hand, receives its energies from that of the heart through the arteries. That is, our tendencies to be attracted to pleasure pass through our veins while our tendencies to avoid pain pass through our arteries. The two together, therefore, act to "attract pleasure" and "avoid pain or harm."

Traditionalists believe that our natural state is one of pleasure whether it be in attracting pleasures or in protecting the pleasure system through the avoiding harm/pain (preserving the individual). If the affective dominates, we are attracted to all sorts of pleasures. If the behavioral system dominates, we are ruled by the urge for power and ambition. This becomes clear in the words of al-Ghazzali:

> Know that however much lust is stronger, the spiritual reward for opposing it is that much greater. There is no appetite stronger than this, but the acting out of this appetite is unseemly. Most of those who do not give rein to this appetite are either unable to, or do not do so out of shame and the fear of disclosure and the ruin of their reputations. There is no spiritual reward for those who abstain for these reasons, for their obedience is motivated by the world, not the Religious Law. And, an inability to commit sins is a blessing , for one will indeed not fall liable to punishment and sin whatever the reason for one's abstinence. However, if a person masters this forbidden thing without any obstacle, and he abstains for the sake of God (*lil-Lah*), his spiritual reward is great. He is one of the seven persons who shall be under the shade of the Throne of God Most High on the Day of Resurrection. His degree will be the degree of Joseph (ﷺ) in that meaning. Joseph (ﷺ) was the imam and leader in negotiating this dangerous passage.[17]

These two systems cooperate in such a way that the actions of the behavioral system unite with or replace those of affect whenever we are in difficulty. When we sense an object to be desirable, affection responds, and from this, in turn, we are motivated because of our desire to possess it. If the object can easily be procured, the affective/attraction to pleasure system supplies sufficient energy—i.e. we are hungry, have food and eat. However, if any obstacles get in the way—i.e., we have no food—the behavioral/avoidance of pain system yields hope in support of the affective system by our action of going to the store to get food, enabling us to strive with greater effort to get the pleasure that we want. Our "attraction to pleasure" power may deprive us of contentment until the obstacle has been removed and our desire satisfied (i.e. we have satisfied our hunger). However, whenever there is an insurmountable problem—i.e. we have no money to buy food—our affective system is overwhelmed with loss of hope so that we do not spend energy in vain.

The same is true in regard to avoidance of pain. Courage leads us to combat that which oppresses us—i.e. we go to war—but fear prevents our persisting against great odds—we submit when overwhelmed. Whenever difficulty afflicts us, our behavioral system supports our emotions or affective system.

The result is far more dangerous to our balance than when our emotional or our behavioral system each act alone. The behavioral system may induce us to pursue that which is contrary to the affective system. It may risk our very life to seek revenge or to be envious. Thus the very means which nature—in its mode of operation—provided to insure the survival of the individual may prove its undoing. The two systems, acting together, can fan into a flame that destroys rationality.

The affective-behavioral systems or animal soul may proceed from a mild state to an extreme one. Desire of a future good may kindle either hope (a mild state) or despair (an extreme state). The resentment of a future event stirs either fear (an extreme state) or courage (a moderate state depending upon the circumstances). The perception of a present evil, which at first caused grief, may incite anger. The progress between emotion and behavior is frequently from grief to anger.

If these two systems dominate, they blind our sense of understanding. They can cause our sense of reason to judge whatever promotes their needs as good and agreeable to reason. The domination of our animal soul (emotion-behavior) can be so strong that our energies are exhausted and their perception, then, prevents us from returning to a normal state.

THE COGNITIVE SYSTEM

Animals also have the animal soul and if we as human beings do not proceed beyond this, we would just be another of the animal species according to al-Ghazzali. We would either be bestial (attraction to pleasure, appetite or lust) or predatory (avoidance of pain, anger). The difference lies in the third system within us—the cognitive system. Al-Ghazzali refers to the positive aspect of cognition, thinking or gaining knowledge as angelic and the negative as satanic. Our cognitive system is the center where our knowledge is stored and out of which our actions should initiate after reflection.

Al-Ghazzali tells us that the animal soul was created earlier than our spiritual heart and took over the breast when we were children.

> First, the animal soul, which is the tool of Satan, was put in control over him. Reason—which is the enemy of the animal soul and is the light of the essence of the angels—was created after the establishment of the animal soul (in him) and the animal soul seized and conquered the fortress of the breast. The animal soul became accustomed to and familiar with the breast (the eventual area of the heart).[18]

Other characteristics of affective or emotional-behavioral response to a situation include contradiction and contrariety. Contradiction and contrariety have to do with our ability to reason. When we least expect it, the two systems may completely undermine our rationality. While we are engaged in thought, an emotion or motion so strong may creep into us that we are carried beyond all control. We have to respond even if it means losing our life. The desires of these systems (the animal soul) neither keep order or measure because of the inability of the animal soul to reflect.

The cognitive system is actualized through nurture. Its final form depends upon the quality and quantity of the environment in which we grow and develop. If our nurturing process is a psychically healthy one, we will actualize our natural disposition for discerning between positive and negative dispositions, good and bad, right and wrong, possible and impossible. This is done through particular guidance in the form of Divine Grace of which we may or may not be aware.

If our nurturing process has been a psychically unhealthy one—in the sense that we were brought up without being taught how to reason—we will lead our "self" astray. In terms of free will actions, an underdevelopment of reason is called a state of preconsciousness, that is, not being present in consciousness, but capable of being "reminded" of it without encountering any resistance or repression, "knowing that you do not know." An undevelopment of reason, a negative trait which is known as the most fatal kind in terms of morality, is unconsciousness. Alienated from self-awareness, unconscious impulses are naturally disposed to be stronger to preserve the human race and the individual when there is no possibility of consciousness (exercise of reason). It is not knowing and not knowing that we do not know. When there is an overdevelopment of reason, hypocrisy, cleverness and identity disturbances take over the self.

Al-Ghazzali frequently warns of the dangers of hypocrisy:

> Another thing is that one must watch one's ani-
> mal soul as the appetite of hypocrisy commonly lies
> hidden inside one. On the pretext of others' follow-
> ing his example he makes (his acts of devotion) pub-
> lic until he is ruined. This weak one is like the per-
> son who does not know how to swim and is about to
> drown. He seizes the hand of another and both per-
> ish.[19]

If guidance comes at a later life stage, we will then make the attempt to implement God's Will and perfect our God-given nature. Al-Ghazzali describes the gradual process to restoring the healthy psychic self:

> . . . he is made habituated to opposing the appetite
> little by little until he becomes bold, for when a per-
> son desires to become strong, he must test his
> strength and perform acts of strength. Little by lit-
> tle and bit by bit he goes farther. A person who
> wants to wrestle with a strong man must first wres-
> tle with persons who are weaker and test his
> strength with them so as to increase (his own)
> strength. It is for this that the strength of people
> who do hard work is greater. The treatment for
> obtaining patience in all affairs is this.[20]

It is then that we will have attained what al-Ghazzali's refers to as the angelic state. This is a process known as "restoration of psychic health." If not, we will live out our life in a state of unconsciousness, unaware of our true potential, never completing the perfection of nature in its mode of oper-ation.

The animal soul becomes accustomed to comfort and ease al-Ghazzali tells us:

Another reason is that when the animal soul becomes accustomed to comfort and ease, it acquires a love for the permitted things of the world and the heart becomes attached to them, turning this world into its heaven. Death becomes difficult. Rudeness and heedlessness appear in one's heart. When he engages in the remembrance (of God) and intimate conversation (with God), he finds no pleasure in it. Not craving lawful desires makes him turn to (love of remembering of God). He becomes discomfited and troubled. The world becomes hateful to him and an eagerness for the comfort of the Hereafter appears in his heart. In a state of sorrow and broken-heartedness, a single glorification will have the effect upon his heart that hundreds (of glorifications) did not have when he was in a state of joy and ease.[21]

As a result, the spiritual heart has to be "weaned" from reliance upon the animal soul al-Ghazzali says:

The similitude of the animal soul is the falcon that is trained by putting it into a chamber and covering its eyes so as to restrain from all that was in it of its falcon-ness. Then, gradually, it will be given meat so that it may become familiar with the falconer and obedient to him. In the same way, the heart does not find intimacy with God Most High so long as you do not wean it from all habits and do not close off the eyes, tongue, and eyes (to such things), and you do not discipline it with seclusion, hunger, silence, and sleeplessness. In the beginning this will be difficult for it—just as when a child is weaned from milk. Afterwards, (the child) will become such that if one tries to give him milk by force, he will not be able to drink it.[22]

Bearing hunger by choice—not by necessity—according to

al-Ghazzali is one of the best ways to learn to control the animal soul.

> Know that the object of hunger is the breaking of the animal soul, bringing it under control, and correcting it. When it is upright, these measures do not become necessary. It is for this reason that while a spiritual guide commands all of this for the disciple, he himself does not do it. The object is not pain and hunger; rather, the object is that he eat that amount which neither makes his stomach heavy nor leaves the feeling of hunger. Both of these distract one from worship. The perfection in this lies in partaking of the attributes of the angels: they experience neither the pain of hunger nor the heaviness of repletion with food. However, the animal soul does not obtain this balance except by applying force to it in the beginning.[23]

If we succeed in becoming conscious and aware of the greater struggle, we will search for balance and equilibrium in the three systems of affect (emotion, lust, attraction to pleasure), behavior (anger, avoidance of pain), and reason according to al-Ghazzali.

> Now you must learn that nothing is pleasant or unpleasant to you so long as you are first not aware of it. Being aware of things is the charge of the senses and reason. The senses are five, and for each one of these there is a pleasure and because of that pleasure one likes it. That is, (your) nature inclines to it: The sensory pleasure of the eye is in beautiful forms and in greenery, flowing water, and the like. It necessarily loves them. The pleasure of the ears is in beautiful and rhythmic voices (and sounds). The pleasure of the nose is in sweet scents. The pleasure of the taste is in foods. The pleasure of touch is in soft touches. All of these are love; that is,

(your) nature has an inclination towards them, and animals have all of these, too.

The sixth sense is something in the heart which is called "reason," called "vision," called "light," or by whatever term you wish to say. It is that which distinguishes a human being from beasts. It also has cognition or perceptions which are pleasant to it and which are dear to it, just as other pleasures are agreeable to the senses and dear to the senses. About this the Messenger (ﷺ) said: "Three things of the world have been made my friend: women, sweet scents, and my delight in formal prayer." He placed the highest degree on formal prayer. Whoever is bestial is unaware of the heart and knows naught but the senses. He will never believe that formal prayer is pleasing and that it may be loved. A person who is dominated by his insight and is more distant from the attributes of the beasts, prefers the observation with the inner eye of the beauty of the Divine Presence, the wonders of His handiwork, the perfection and majesty of His Essence and Attributes over the observations with the outer eye of fine forms and greenery and flowing water; indeed, in his view all of these become lowly after the beauty of the Divine presence has been revealed to him.[24]

3 Therefore, you must seek out the truth about yourself: What sort of a thing are you? Where did you come from? Where are you going? Why have you come to this stopping place? For what purpose were you created? What is your happiness and in what does it lie? What is your misery and in what does that lie?

What sort of a thing are you? al-Ghazzali asks. Throughout the *Alchemy* he cautions about being arrogant.

The point of this that you should not call yourself one of the chosen of the Divine Presence so that
you measure everything according to yourself and
you say about that in which there is no benefit (for
you): "Why was this created? There is no purpose in
it!" When you have understood that the ant was not
created for you, know that the moon, the sun, the
stars, the heavens, and the angels, all of these also
were not created for you, even though you have
some benefit from them; just as the fly was not created for you, even though you have some benefit
from it. For it has been chosen to eat all that is
unpleasant to you and would putrefy, in order to
lessen the unpleasant stench. The butcher was not
created for the fly, even though there is a benefit
from him for the fly. Your supposition that the sun
rises for your sake every day is like the supposition
of the fly that imagines that the butcher goes to his
shop every day for its sake so that it will be able to
eat its fill of blood and unpleasantnesses. Just as a
butcher himself turns to other work so that he does
not remember the fly, even though the leavings of
his work is the life and sustenance of the fly, the
sun is turned to the service of the Divine Presence
in its circumambulations and movements and does
not remember you, even though the leavings of its
light enables your eyes to see and the earth is tem-
pered by the leavings of its temperament so that
the plants which are your food grow. Therefore,
there is for us in the purpose of creation that which
has no connection with you. . . .[25]

We are in one sense a series of powers or abilities as al-
Ghazzali describes us:

Know that powers have been created in the
human being: each one created for a purpose and in
consistency with his nature. Its pleasure is consis-

tent with his nature, just as the power of anger has been created for dominance and revenge and one's pleasure is in (doing) that. The power of lust has been created for the obtaining of nourishment and one's pleasure is in (doing) that. Make an analogy of the faculties of hearing, sight, etc., in the same manner: each one has a pleasure and these pleasures are different. The pleasure of sexual intercourse is different from the pleasure of giving rein to one's anger. There are also differences in strength; some are stronger, as the pleasure of the eye from a fine image is more dominant than the pleasure of the nose in pleasant scents. A power has also been created in the human being which is called "reason" and "illumination." It was created for the knowledge and gnosis which do not enter the imagination or the senses, and that is his nature, too. One's pleasure in that is that by it one knows that this world has been created and it requires a wise and All-Powerful Planner Who always was. In the same way, one learns the attributes of the Maker and His wisdom in (His) creation.[26]

Where did you come from?

OUR BODY CREATED FROM THE ELEMENTS

The elements, in the traditional perspective, develop in the atmosphere between the moon and the earth. Once on earth, they are preserved in the mineral "soul" or nature in its mode of operation as the Will of God. The elements are earth, air, fire, and water. Earth is dry and cold, water is cold and moist, air is hot and moist, and fire is hot and dry. Earth is the opposite of air and water is the opposite of fire. Union is possible because water acts as an intermediary between earth and air and air acts as an intermediary between water and fire.

The elements possess the natural disposition to ascend, descend, and to move in a circular direction. Each element is joined by one of its qualities to that which is below it and above it—water to earth below it by coldness and water to air above by moisture; air to water below it by moisture and to fire above it by heat; fire to air below it by heat and to earth, towards which it inclines in a circular motion, by dryness; earth to water above it by coldness and to fire, which declines towards it, by dryness. The elements are continually produced one from the other and their energy is never lost. The movement of the elements produce the humors within which, in turn, one's natural temperament is determined.

Two other functions these qualities have is that of being active or passive. Heat and cold are active while moisture and dryness are passive. Heat and cold are considered active because sometimes they draw on moisture and sometimes on dryness. A correspondence also exists between fire and understanding, air and reason, water and imagination and earth and the external senses where the four qualities are again repeated: fire is likened to sight, air to hearing, water to taste and smell and earth to feeling.

Animals and we human beings inherit the natural dispositions of the mineral and plant soul as nature in its mode of operation and two special natural dispositions of their own, namely, voluntary motivation and perception by organs.

Al-Ghazzali recommends that we meditate upon our self.

> So, meditate upon yourself at first as to whence (you came). At first He created you from a droplet of fluid, and He made the first residence for that droplet the loins of your father and the womb of your mother. He made earth of your mother's womb and He made a seed from your father's spine. After that, He made the seed of your creation. Then He appointed passion to the male and female so that

the seed would be sown in the earth. Then He made the menstrual blood irrigate that seed and created you from a drop of semen and menstrual blood. First, some blood congeals, then it becomes flesh, that which is called the fetus. Then, He breathed life into it. Then, from that simple blood and liquid He caused a multitude of things to appear in you such as skin, flesh, veins, sinews, and bones. Then from all of these, He gave form to your limbs. He created a round head, two long arms and long legs and at the end of each (limb) five branches. Then, on the exterior, He created eyes, ears, a mouth, a nose, a tongue and the other organs; and inside you, the stomach, the kidneys, the liver, the spleen, the gall bladder, the bladder, and the plentiful intestines. Each one has its own shape and its own attribute, and has a different size. He divided each of these into several parts. Each finger as three joints, and each member is composed of flesh, skin, veins, fat, and bones. He created your eye, not larger in size than a walnut, in seven layers, each layer possessing a special quality. If one of them fails, the world becomes dark for you. If we were to expound on the marvels of the eye alone, many pages would be blackened (with ink).

Then, look at your own skeleton and how He created a hard and firm solid from a delicate and thin liquid. Every part of it has its own shape and size; some (bones) are round, some are long, some are broad, some are hollow, and some are solid, each one is mounted on the other. In the size, shape, and appearance of each there is a wisdom; rather, there are many wisdoms. Then He made the bones the pillars of the body and He built everything upon them. If (the skeleton) were one piece, you would not be able to bend your spine; if it were in scattered loosely about, you would not be able to hold your spine straight or stand upon your feet. So He created it in segments so that it could bend. Then

He put it together and wound sinews and veins on it and made it strong; then He made it like a single unit to stand erect when needed. On each vertebra (of the spine) He brought out four projections like swellings and in the vertebra beneath it four depressions like hollows so that that projections would be seated in the hollows and stand firm. From the sides of the vertebrae He brought out projections so that the sinews could be wound about them, to strengthen them so that one rests upon another. He made your whole skull of fifty-five pieces of bone and bound them together with fine seams so that if one part is damaged the others will be sound and all will not be broken. He created teeth, some with broad crowns to grind food, and others with thin and sharp crowns to cut and break up food and (then) pass (the pieces) to the molars. Then He created seven vertebrae for the neck with veins and sinews tightly wound about them and mounted the head upon them. He created the spine of twenty-four vertebrae and placed the neck on it. He inserted the broad ribs in these vertebrae, and the same for the other bones, the description of which would be lengthy. In sum, He created two hundred and forty-eight bones in your body, each one with a special purpose so that your affair would be correct and prepared. He created all of this out of that despicable fluid. If one of those bones were missing, you would be rendered helpless; if there were one more of them, you would (also) be helpless.[27]

PERCEPTION

With the development of the animal soul, our sense of perception begins to operate to distinguish images from objects in reality. Perception as a function of animals consists of five external and internal sensible and psychic senses.

FIVE EXTERNAL SENSES

The five external senses are the abilities to see, hear, taste, touch and smell. These external senses are each capable of a basic perception of things that are actually present to the external sense organs. Their perception, however, is based on a single kind of impression.

FIVE INTERNAL SENSES

The five inner senses are the abilities to have common sense, imagination, representation, rational perception and memory.

COMMON SENSE

Common sense, the first internal sense, is the storehouse for all impressions from the outer world. It directly receives the contents of the five external senses. For instance, when an apple is perceived, through "common" sense, we distinguish the different states of the apple and realize that every part of the apple possesses taste, smell, color, warmth, or cold.

There are four functions connected to common sense: to receive an impression; to act on it as arbiter of reports from the five external senses; to transmit the results to a more inward sense; to reduce contrary images to a unity of perception thereby destroying false impressions which may arise from several impressions received at the same time from different senses. It is the most basic sense of internal perception. Second is the internal sense of retaining forms or representation. This comes into action after common sense has stopped. It stores and retains the forms received by common sense. Third is sensible/rational imagination.

Perception is of three types: sensible, psychic, and cognitive/rational. The sensible functions include external and internal senses. Psychic and cognitive perception can be processed, as well, through the internal senses alone.

Although common sense, representation, and sensible imagination are held in common by animals and us, there are differences because of the human capacity for rationality.

REPRESENTATION

Representation receives images that have been received and sorted by the common sense. Its main function within the self is to continue the thought process, to recommend important forms to the deliberations of rational imagination and to store them in memory. It retains impressions longer than common sense does and tries them in balance.

IMAGINATION

While being referred to as sensible imagination in animals, imagination forms the basis of psychical perception. Whereas sensible perception is particular, imagination is general and it culminates in cognitive or rational perception so that it is the intermediary between the sensible and the rational. It is active while we are both awake and asleep and is the cause of dreams. It can operate out of either the immediate experience of intuition or out of the deliberations of reason.

As soon as the rational sense makes distinctions of universal meanings and presents them to our sense of reason to look more closely into them through the insight of our ability to reason, our sense of reason looks at them through the image which the imaginative sense represents. The our sense of reason or rational sense distinguishes whether the image is perfect or not perfect, common or not common. It thinks immediately of the intelligible meanings. This is the way that universal meanings are understood by artists and scientists. When the artist, for example, thinks about how to make an object, he presents the image of the particular article to his imagination and prepares his plan to make it. Similarly, when a scientist looks into the object of knowledge to know its nature and give its description, he presents its image to his imagination.

Imagination writes in memory impressions of things received by the five external senses as well as by reason in addition to things it composes itself. It is like a person who writes himself a note to remind himself of something and later reads the note and mentally adds something from his mind at that moment to the note. Later imagination may return to the forms and activate them without the intervention of the external senses. In this case, it is activated by the affective or behavioral systems attracting us to pleasure or avoiding harm. It has also been noted that imagination is more likely to follow the senses than to follow reason. Once the senses are satiated, imagination is free to busy itself with other forms. Imagination is never idle. It often leads us to confusion.

It is quite possible for our imagination to oppose reason. Since it is closer to the external senses than it is to reason, it may allure us to the affective or behavioral systems to establish a coalition against reason. Rash judgments are strengthened in this way.

Imagination plays a crucial role in us. It develops ideals and is naturally disposed to pass those that are of sufficient magnitude onto reason for deliberation. It also communicates with the spiritual heart where the energy of the affective-behavioral systems or animal soul resides. It has to do with both thought and action. It receives sense impressions before it can respond. Imagination has considerable authority over our "self." Because of its freedom and its dual relation to reason and the affective-behavioral systems or animal soul, it exercises an important influence on conduct which may not be to our best advantage in trying to center our "self" as it is considered that right conduct comes from reason.

COGNITIVE/RATIONAL PERCEPTION

The fourth internal sense marks cognitive or rational perception within us. Cognition may be achieved in two basic ways: first through discursive reasoning, deliberation, and drawing conclusions. This is referred to as reason or rationality. The second type of cognition is that of direct awareness or experience and is referred to as intuition, its extension being gnosis. With the latter, cognition is attained without learning or making an effort to acquire cognition.

Making up the fourth internal sense, intuition/reason can operate without any sensible impressions. As reason, this type of internal perception is inclined towards the deduction of sciences, crafts, and the perception of intelligibles. Just as sensible imagination contained the ability to perceive information from the external senses and motivate attraction to pleasure and avoidance of harm, so, also, reason has a perceptive ability and a motivational one. Its perceptive ability is that of deliberation and understanding. Its motivating force is that of will power.

These two—conscience and will power—are referred to as the practical intellect. As the final point in an act, the practical intellect receives and illuminates ideas that have come from our imagination. It also has a reflective power by which it examines its own actions and certain innate criteria which provide knowledge of universal and practical guidance. Because of these natural dispositions, we not only comprehend particular forms, but are also able to distinguish between positive and negative dispositions and ultimately to arrive at Divine Truth.

Reason is used when our intellect considers material things and understanding is used by which universal, spiritual truths are comprehended. When reason strives towards contemplation, it is called the cognitive intellect. When it seeks the positive and having found it goes forward to the will in order that we may follow the positive or flee from the negative, it is called the practical intellect which contains the Active Intellect within itself. It is also referred to as wisdom. From each of the functions a habit of life may develop—contemplative or active. The word active is used in regard to the practical intellect because it does not stop with the discovery of a positive or negative trait but goes forward with the will.

MEMORY AND/OR RECALL

The fifth sense is that of memory or recall. Natural dispositions are held in storage here which we only need to be reminded of to recall. It does not, however, hold the forms gathered by common sense and retained by the second internal sense.

MOTIVATION

In addition to perception, we also contain a motivational system as part of the animal soul. Motivation, including will power, renders us capable of action. Motivation is of two types: the first gives an impulse requiring a voluntary response and the second involuntarily causes the body to react on its own accord. When a pleasurable or painful image is imprinted on the internal sense called sensible imagination, it rouses us to movement. This impulsive arousal has two subdivisions.

As previously stated, these two naturally disposed, unconscious/ preconscious functions within our animal soul make-up its two basic systems. Known in philosophy as the concupiscible or attraction to pleasure and irascible or avoidance of pain, in psychological terms they are referred to as "attraction to pleasure" or "the pleasure principle" and "avoidance of pain" or "the pain principle." They are essentially the unconscious, affective/emotive and the preconscious, behavioral systems.

Our voluntary motivation contains, in addition to the

properties of animal motivation, free-will. It is the highest form of motivation in nature's mode of operation and is independent of conscience or reason. It may do as it pleases, our spiritual heart will be held responsible in the Hereafter for our intentions or motivations for the choices we make.

OUR COGNITIVE SYSTEM

The cognitive system is the control center for thought and actions of our conscience, free-will, and ability to gain consciousness of our "self." The norm in traditional psychology is for the cognitive system to regulate the preconscious (not to the extent that it can come to know, but to the extent that it can be disciplined) behavioral and unconscious affective natural dispositions by keeping them in a state of equilibrium or moderation in terms of the Straight Path.

THE INTELLECT
THE PRACTICAL INTELLECT

We are also equipped through universal guidance with what is known as the practical intellect as part of the process of nature in its mode of operation.

Whenever we intend to create something, we first form an image of it in our practical intellect (conscience and free will) which transfers it to the internal sense of imagination. We then set the organs into motion to bring it into being. Our practical intellect understands and abstracts in imagination.

When our practical intellect operates out of the internal sense of imagination, it abstracts the image of the thing to be created according to a particular form or size. Self-motivation then moves the organs to create the object. Thus it is the practical intellect which first creates the thing and not self-motivation of the organs. The self is naturally disposed to motivation but only does so in the Creative Act when the practical intellect causes the thing to be created to appear in the internal sense of imagination. Only after that does self-motivation cause the things to be created by the use of the organs.

The practical intellect, then, has two functions: to present to the internal sense of imagination the image of the thing to be created; and to have the thing come into being outside the self by motivating the organs of the body.

It is through our practical intellect that we love or hate, live in society, and have friends and positive dispositions. The practical intellect is the locus of the highest forms of perception and motivation. The highest form of nature in its mode of operation in the perceptive system within the self is the conscience which is the source of the general principles upon which morality is based. The highest form of nature in its mode of operation in the voluntary motivational system is choice or free-will. It receives sensible and cognitive stimuli from the external and internal senses. When the stimuli are purely sensible, they have been first passed from the senses to the attraction to pleasure or avoidance of harm systems and from there to the practical intellect where a response is given. When the stimuli are purely cognitive, they pass directly into the practical intellect for action. When the stimuli are both sensible and cognitive, the practical intellect is the locus of operation for deliberation and the production of some action including human arts and sciences. The practical intellect contains the cognitive intellect and the latter develops through four stages.

THE COGNITIVE INTELLECT

There are four stages in the acquiring of the cognitive intellect which is held in preparedness within the practical intellect. Each one is called an intellect. Once the practical intellect acquires these intellects by completing the perfection of nature in its mode of operation within the self, that is, when the self is centered, the practical intellect then operates through the Active Intellect. The four stages are: potential, habitual, Active, and acquired intellects.

At the first stage of the potential intellect, the self thinks nothing but is prepared to think. Here the intellect cannot be creative in the act of knowledge. It is simply receptive to it. If there is actual knowledge at this stage, we will not understand the reality of it. Out of this, through "reminders" grows the habitual intellect. Here the possibility of actualizing the potential intellect's preparedness exists. This means knowing the principles or axioms of knowledge like the whole is greater than the sum of its parts. The Active Intellect is the stage when we no longer need a physical form. It is solely concerned with intellectual demonstrations and is either acquired or bestowed as a Divine Gift. The Active Intellect, the center of all forms of thought, has a natural disposition by which it can reflect and then perform the act of thinking. It also has a reflective power by which it examines its own actions and certain criteria of its natural disposition which provides a knowledge of the law of God and nature. By virtue of these naturally disposed notions, we not only comprehend particular and material forms, but, also, as a result of several processes, distinguish between positive and negative traits and arrive ultimately at universal and Divine truths. The Active Intellect operates through three stages: exercise of deliberation; exercise of conscience; drawing conclusions.

Finally there is the acquired intellect which is the highest stage of the intellects. These stages are like signs upon the way of centering of self and beyond. The traveler is always our "self." At the stage of the acquired intellect, every conceptual form potentially contained in us becomes apparent to us like the face of a person reflected in a mirror held before us.

Here acquisition ceases. All the forms exist in the cognitive intellect, held within the practical intellect, which is in a state where we can perform the act of thinking which occurs when the Active Intellect causes the habitual intellect to reflect back on itself and through this process, we begins to think about the forms we have.

The cognitive intellect, then, is concerned with the cognition of truth. The objects that this natural disposition deals with are necessary, universal, and unchangeable like mathematical properties. They can be contemplated, but not deliberated for there is only one truth. The cognitive intellect is the part of the perceptive system where forms are imprinted. If the form exists in matter, it abstracts them. If they are already abstract, it receives them. It is located within the practical intellect.

The Process of Activating Thought/Action

The process of thought in which action results, according to traditional psychology, can be described in the following way. When an object is perceived by the external senses (seeing, hearing, tasting, touching, smelling), nervous energy enables each organ effected to receive a particular kind of impression to which it has been naturally disposed to adapt. The impressions are sometimes vague and may be contradictory. Nervous energy hastens to the locus of common sense where the impressions of the external senses are reduced to a unity and stored in the internal sense of representation which continues the thought process and gives the image to the internal sense of imagination.

This internal sense, having been able to elaborate ideas because of the nervous energy it has received, may assign the images to memory or may recommend them to reason and understanding before storing them for future use. If action is required, our imagination communicates to our spiritual heart informing it about the pleasure or pain of the object. At the same instant, the images or ideas, compounded by the imagination from their original, simple impressions, are abstracted and perceived by our sense of reason. Reason deliberates and draws a conclusion which it presents to our free will as positive or negative. Our free will, being the final decision maker, then decides to accept or reject the counsel of reason. The affective-behavioral systems (or animal soul) obey our free will and set to work those things necessary for action. They command us to motion to attract the pleasure or avoid pain.

This is the procedure for thought/action when our cognitive system is in balance. If our nurturing process has not been oriented towards preserving a healthy moral self, reason's advice will not be accepted by our free will. Our free will may even be bypassed by the affective-behavioral systems and respond to imagination themselves, singularly or together, in commanding the self to action.

Our external-internal senses involved in sensible perception are naturally disposed to cooperate in such a way that each lower sense provides an image or stimulus adequate to the needs of the sense directly above it. Impressions received by the external senses become increasingly "abstracted" and "purified of the sensible," passing through our psychical perception of imagination until they culminate in the cognitive system's positive disposition of wisdom. Thus our knowledge passes through several levels from the single sensible impression of each one of the external senses involved, through psychical perception, to the extent of spiritual truths. We then understand many things which are beyond impressions provided by the external senses, from which the our spirit of self is moved just as the external senses are moved by external objects.

The knowledge that we receive from the external senses is like shadows of them. The knowledge we have from common sense, representation, and imagination is as if we looked upon the images with more clarity than their shadows. The knowledge we have of understanding is as if we viewed not only the shadows and clear images of things, but also their very presence. The knowledge we have by reason is as if in addition to the shadow, clear image, and presence of an object, we saw its effects as well so that the nature of the object as it really is may be known.

Perception, then evolves ideas in various stages of completion. The degree of perception is accompanied by a corresponding degree of motivation. First is our perception from the external senses which our nervous energy presents to our organs to give us elementary knowledge of an object from which we receive a stimulus. This perception is limited. For instance, if an object perceived is too large, our sight needs the help of the internal senses. None of the external senses, without the help of imagination and memory, can build up impressions.

Next come psychical impressions in our imagination which have no external form or abstract images of to understand to then will some response. Each of these may give rise to an attraction to pleasure or avoidance of pain response.

The structure of our "self" develops out of nature in its mode of operation in the mineral, plant, and animal. It shares the elements and their qualities with minerals; assimilative, reproductive, and growth functions with the plant; and perception and motivation with animals. We begin to distinguish our "self" from the animal at the level of the third internal sense where we can employ free will to obey God's Will while the animal has no choice. It has to obey God's Will.

Out of our motivation comes our attraction to pleasure and avoidance of harm as well as our free will. Out of our perception our conscience is illuminated. Our practical intellect evolves out of the combination of perception and motivation. Out of the practical intellect, the cognitive intellect develops. When our practical intellect is served by conscience, will power and understanding, it reflects on us through the presence of the Active Intellect and we become conscious of self. Our practical intellect is then called our Active Intellect. In order to be more certain that centering will be attained, al-

Ghazzali says the natural way is for our Active Intellect to consciously make our will power choose that which is more difficult. This way we can be more assured that we are allowing the cognitive system to regulate. But even then, according to traditional psychology, the only way to be sure of being centered is through receiving Divine Grace (right guidance, confirmation and support).

The appearance of our Active Intellect marks the beginning of our greater struggle. Once centered, it is our Active Intellect operating out of the internal sense of imagination, by-passing reason and deliberation, that regulates us as we move as a spiraling center on the conscious return to the Source.

Where are you going?

Al-Ghazzali says that we are going either to heaven or hell and describes our sojourn on earth as a business transaction.

> So, the wise and the great ones of religion have realized that they have come into this world to engage in business, and the transactions are with the self. The profit or loss of these transactions is heaven and hell; rather, it is eternal happiness and misery. Therefore, one's self is put in the position of a business partner: just as with a partner conditions are made, then he is watched, and then he is audited. If he has been treacherous, he will be punished or reproved. So, (the wise and the saints), too, have stood with their selves in these six stations: (1) On Fixing Mutual Conditions, (2) On Vigilance, (3) On Reckoning, (4) On Punishment, (5) On Striving, and (6) On Reproac-hing."[28]

Why are you here?

Al-Ghazzali sees the reason for being here is to love God.

Know that love is a valuable jewel. Claiming love is easy so that a person may think that he is one of the lovers; but there are signs and proofs of love. One must seek the signs in oneself, and they are seven:

(1) The first is that there is no loathing of death, for no friend dislikes the sight of the Friend. The Messenger (饟) said: "Whoever loves the sight of God Most High, God Most High loves the sight of him, too." Buwayti said to one of the ascetics: "Do you love death?" The ascetic hesitated in replying. (Buwayti) said: "If you were truthful, you would love it." However, it is permissible that there be love and loathing at the hastening of death—(but) not at the principle of death—so that one who has not yet prepared his provisions (for the Hereafter) may make (them). The sign of this is that one is impatient in preparing the provisions.

(2) The second sign is that one prefers what is loved by God Most High over what is loved by oneself. He does not neglect anything he knows to be the cause of his nearness to the Beloved. He avoids all that causes his distancing (himself) from that. This is a person who loves God Most High with all his heart. As the Messenger (饟) said: "Say to whoever wishes to see a person who loves God with all his heart: 'Look at Salim, the client of Hudhayfah.'"

Moreover, if a person commits a sin, it does not follow that he is not a lover (of God); instead, his love is not with his whole heart. The evidence of this is that Nuayman was punished several times for drinking wine. Someone cursed him in the presence of the Messenger (饟). The Messenger (饟) said: "Curse him not, for he loves God Most High and His Messenger." Fudayl said: "When you are asked if you love God, remain silent. If you say 'no,' you become an unbeliever; if you say 'yes,' your behavior does not resemble the acts of the lovers (of God)."

(3) The third sign is that one always renews the remembrance of God Most High in one's heart and is eager to do that without taking pains; for whoever loves a thing remembers it frequently. If the love is complete, one never forgets (the object of love) itself. Yet, if one must force the heart to remember, it is feared that his beloved is that His remembrance dominate his heart. Consequently, it may be that the love for God Most High is not dominant, but the love for the love of Him dominates him who desires to love. Love is one thing and the love of love is another.

(4) The fourth sign is that one loves the Quran, which is His Word, and the Messenger (ﷺ) and all that is established by Him. When the loves has become strong, one loves all mankind, for all are His servants; indeed, one loves all extant things, for all are His creation, just as one who loves someone loves his composition and writing.

(5) The fifth sign is that one is avid for intimate conversation (with God) in private and desirous for the coming of night. Crowds and hindrances depart and one holds conversation with the Friend in private. If one prefers sleep and idle chatter to solitude during the night and the day, one's love is weak. Revelation came to David (ﷺ): "O David, become the intimate of no one among mankind. No one is cut off from Me save two persons: one is he who hastens in the search for spiritual reward. When it comes late to him, he becomes languid. The other is he who forgets Me and is satisfied with his own condition. The sign of that is that I leave him alone and I keep him bewildered in the world."

So, if love is total, affection for nothing else remains. There was a worshippers among the Children of Israel who would perform his formal prayer at night. He would perform his formal prayer beneath a tree where a bird with a sweet voice would sing. Revelation came to the messenger of the era: "Tell him: 'You have become accustomed to seclusion; your degree has fallen because you are not attending to anything of that.'"

Some have achieved such a degree in their conversations (with God) that fire has broken out in the other side of the dwelling and they were not be aware of it! The foot of one of them was cut during (his) formal prayer on some pretext, and he was unaware of it. Revelation came to David (ﷺ): "A person who claimed to love Me lied and slept all night; does the friend not desire the sight of the Friend? Whoever seeks me, I am with him." Moses (ﷺ) said: "O Lord God, where art Thou that I may seek Thee? He answered: "Whenever thou hast intended to seek (Me), thou hast found (Me)."

(6) The sixth sign is that worship becomes easy for one and its burdensomeness falls away. Someone says: "For twenty years I forced myself to perform the night formal prayer; afterwards, I have taken delight in that for twenty years." When love becomes strong, no pleasure equals the pleasure of worship; how can it itself be difficult?

(7) The seventh sign is that one loves all of His devout servants and one is merciful and compassionate to them, and one holds all unbelievers and rebels (against God) in enmity. As He said: *(They are) hard against the disbelievers and merciful among themselves.* (Q. 48:29) One of the prophets asked: "O Lord God, who are Thy saints and friends?" He answered: "Those who are captivated with Me like small children are captivated with their mothers. And just as a bird takes refuge in its nest, they take refuge with the remembrance of Me. Just as a leopard becomes enraged and fears nothing, they become enraged when a person commits a sin."

These and signs like these are many. They are present in him whose love is complete. The love of him who has some of them in him is in accordance with that (amount).[29]

For what purpose were you created?

One answer al-Ghazzali gives is to be a lover of goodness.

> Know that since love is the greatest of the sta-
> tions, becoming acquainted with the remedy for
> achieving it is important. For whoever desires to
> become a lover of goodness, the first step is that one
> turn away from all things except (the beloved).
> Then one continuously looks upon (the beloved).
> When one sees (only the beloved's) face, but the
> hands, feet, and hair are concealed—and that is
> also good—one strives to see (the rest) also, so that
> every beauty one sees will increase one's inclina-
> tion. If one is persevering, the inclination will
> appear in one, small or great.
>
> So, the love for God Most High is also thus. The
> first condition is that one turn one's face away from
> the world and cleanse one's heart from loving it, for
> the love for other than God Most High will distract
> (one) from the love for Him. This is like cleaning the
> ground of thorns and weeds. Then, one seeks the
> gnosis (*marifat*) of Him; for, the cause of anyone's
> not loving Him is that he has not come to know
> Him. If that (were) not so, (His) beauty and perfec-
> tion would naturally be beloved. . . . Obtaining gno-
> sis is like putting a seed in the soil. Then, one con-
> tinually occupies oneself in remembrance (of God)
> and meditation. This is like watering (the seed); for
> whoever remembers a person much, will certainly
> find an intimacy with him.[30]

In what does your happiness lie? In what does your misery lie?

According to al-Ghazzali one sign of happiness is repentance and one sin of misery is sin.

> Whoever has understood the true nature of the
> heart and what the manner of its connection to the

body is, its relationship to the Divine Presence, and what the cause of the veil between it and the (Divine Presence) is, one does not doubt that sin is the cause of the veil and repentance is the cause of acceptance; for the heart is, in its origin, a pure essence of the essence of the angels. It is a like a mirror in which the Divine Presence shows Itself when, upon departure from this world, (the heart) has not been tarnished. With every sin one commits, a darkness is deposited upon the mirror of the heart; and with every act of devotion, a light attaches itself to it and drives off that darkness from it.

The effects of the lights of devotion and the darkness of sins are continually following another one another in the mirror. When the darkness has become great and one has repented, the lights of devotion eliminate the darkness. The heart returns to its clarity and purity. However, if one is so stubborn in one's sinning that the tarnish has reached the essence of the self, and penetrated it deeply, it will not be receptive to treatment any more. It is like the mirror which has been corroded by tarnish. Such a person is itself unable to repent, except by (uselessly) uttering with the tongue: "I have repented.[31]

Our happiness also lies in being proactive in the battle between our angelic and satanic forces according to al-Ghazzali:

As a result, there is continuous warfare and opposition between these two armies (our angelic possibilities vs. the satanic); one says: "Do it!" while the other says: "Do not do it!" One remains continually between these two importuning (forces). If the religious impulse is dug in firmly in the battle with lust and is steadfast, its steadfastness is called patience. Therefore, that is the meaning of patience. If it overcomes lust and repulses it, its triumph is called "victory." While the battle continues in him, this is called "the greater struggle against the animal soul" or ego. So, the meaning of patience is the religious impulse's remaining firm in opposition against lust. Wherever these two opposing armies are not present, there is no patience. This is because there is no need of patience for the angels, while beasts and children do not themselves have the power of patience.

. . . .The point is that you know that patience is a battlefield, and a battlefield is a place where there are two opposing armies. These two armies—one is the angelic cavalry and the other is the satanic cavalry—are gathered in the human breast. Therefore, the first step in the way of religion is involving oneself in this battle, for the satanic hosts have seized the field of the breast in childhood, and the angelic hosts have appeared at the approach of puberty. Consequently, so long as one has not triumphed over one's lust, one will not achieve his (spiritual) happiness; so long as one does not fight and is not steadfast in battle, one will not prevail. Whoever does not involve himself in this war is he who has surrendered his guardianship to Satan. And whoever has controlled his lust and made it obedient to the Religious Law has prevailed over it, is as the Messenger (ﷺ) said: "God aided me in the battle with Satan so that (Satan) surrendered to me." Usually one is engaged in the greater struggle; one time there is victory, another time defeat; one time lust prevails, and another time the religious impulse. That fortress will not be conquered save with patience and steadfastness.[32]

As one obtains victory in the battle within, al-Ghazzali points out that one's longing for God increases bringing greater spiritual happiness.

So you must recognize the meaning of longing, what longing for God Most High is; for there is no love without longing. But one by whom this is not recognized at all, has no longing. If it is recognized, is present, and is seen; it is also not longing. Therefore longing is for something which is present in one respect and absent in another; like the beloved who is present in the imagination, but absent from the eye. The meaning of longing is "request" and "seeking" for that to become present in the eye so that perception may become complete. Then, from this you come to know that it is not possible for the longing for God Most High to be fulfilled in this world. It is present in gnosis (*marifat*), but absent from witnessing. Witnessing is the perfection of gnosis, just as seeing is the perfection of the imagination.[33]

4 As for those attributes which are gathered inside you: some are the attributes of beasts of burden, some are the attributes of predatory animals, some are the attributes of satanic forces, and some are the attributes of the angels. Which of these is you? Which is the truth of your essential nature, while the others are foreign and borrowed? If you do not know this, you cannot seek your own happiness, because for each of these there is a different nutriment and a different happiness.

Whereas in the first three paragraphs of the Prolegomena, al-Ghazzali places emphasis on knowledge, here at paragraph four, five and six, it is more about his second fundamental—states—and its aspect of will power, that which gives to or withholds energy from the self or without it.

According to al-Ghazzali, while we have bestial (lust, attraction to pleasure), predatory (anger, avoidance of pain) and satanic tendencies (hypocrisy, envy, greed, etc.) within us, we also have angelic qualities. The choice we make as to what character we want to have is based on our free will.

Al-Ghazzali describes two angels in particular—conscience and will power. He calls conscience and will power the religious impulse and lust and anger (the animal soul) in their various levels as satanic powers. This, then, is another battle of the greater struggle against the same enemy—religious impulse (the angelic hosts of conscience and will power) against the animal soul (satanic hosts, i.e. lust and anger):

> Moreover, at first a human being is created in the character of the beasts, and the craving for food, clothing, decoration, amusement, and play have been made dominant over him. Then, at the time of puberty a light from the angelic lights appears in him and he sees the results of affairs in that light. Indeed, two angels have been appointed over him, of which the beasts are deprived. One angel (conscience) guides him and shows him the way by means of a light which spreads to him from the lights of the angel so that he recognizes the end of affairs and sees the prudence of affairs until he comes to know himself and God Most High by that light. He understands that end result of the animal soul (lust, pleasure and anger, pain) is total destruction, even if there be delight at the moment. He understands that his pleasure and ease are quickly transitory while his sorrow will be long-lasting. This guidance is not for the beasts.[34] . . . .

Our conscience operates out of our practical intellect. Our practical intellect is the place of our conscience. It is a natural disposition in us and exists to some extent in animals who are naturally disposed to know that their very survival depends on them staying with the mean, on the Straight Path. Our conscience is also naturally predisposed but because of our free will, we are free to accept or reject the advice of our conscience. Al-Ghazzali, then turns to free will or will power.

> However, this guidance is not sufficient; for if one learns that (something) causes loss and that one does not possess the power to ward it off, what is the benefit? A sick person knows that the disease is harmful to him, but he is unable to repulse it. Therefore, God, may be He be praised, has appointed the other angel over him (will power) to give him strength and power and to support and direct him so that he will refrain from that which he has learned is harmful to him. As it is his need that he control his lusts, something else must appear in him to oppose that in order to escape harm in the future. This compulsion for opposition is that of the angelic hosts, while the compulsion to give rein to the animal soul is that of the demonic hosts. This compulsion to oppose the animal soul is what we call the religious impulse, and the compulsion to give rein to our impulsive desires we call the carnal impulse.[35]

God has given us the instrument to be able to overcome the negative tendencies (lust, attraction to pleasure, bestial, and anger, avoidance of pain, predatory as well as imagination in the service of lust and anger or satanic forces within) and that is through our free will power.

Our free will is the highest developed form of motivation in nature's mode of operation. It is naturally disposed by universal guidance to be fair and just as well as to avoid conflict. When our nurturing process is oriented towards preserving our moral health, our free will is gradually trained to accept the counsel of cognition (thinking and reasoning). Cognition, as has been mentioned, contains both the cognitive and practical intellect.

Through habit, our free will has learned to seek the counsel of cognition before making a decision. Our free will deliberates, comes to an understanding of the situation and draws a conclusion. Our free will is then free to accept or reject the conclusion. However, as our free will has a choice, it makes the final decision. Our ability to reason is only a guide, a counselor. Our free will is naturally disposed to be higher than our ability to reason.

Al-Ghazzali points out:

> So long as he is subservient to his free will and that which it does is not in accordance to the rule of the Religious Law, he is following his lusts; his behavior is not that of a servant of God. His (spiritual) happiness lies in his servitude.[36]

If our free will accepts the advice, we regulate our "self" (body, spirit, soul, heart) in a state of balance and harmony, centered in positive dispositions like temperance, courage, and wisdom. If another benefits from this centeredness, we have attained the highest of the positive dispositions, that of being fair and just towards the Creator, the self, nature, and others.

Free-will Rebels Against Reason

When our nurturing process has not fostered the development of a healthy moral self, we have not been nurtured to operate out of reason. Instead, we operate out of the locus of intuition through imagination.

The process is explained like this: our free will seeks the advice of our reason. Our reason responds through our imagination, an internal sense, as has been shown, that is more firmly connected to our animal soul (affective/behavioral systems) than to reason (the cognitive system). The irrational alliance of our free will and animal soul (affect-behavior or lust, anger) combine to force our ability to reason (our cognitive system) to begin to rationalize and legitimize desires that our animal soul (lust and anger, the affective-behavioral systems) could never conceive. We develop what is called over-consciousness.

In this situation, instead of our free will exercising its natural disposition to fairness and justice, our free will falls under its stronger natural disposition to avoid conflict. In doing so, our free will loses its own liberty and freedom, allowing unconscious and preconscious forces to dominate it. Since the animal soul (affect-behavior systems, lust and anger, attraction to pleasure and avoidance of pain) are not capable of consciousness, they are not able to regulate us, but can dominate over our free will.

Our free will often refuses the advice of our reason just to show that it is free. Everything depends on the decision of our free will. Our reason is only a guide. Our free will, then, is subject to a kind of depravity which extends to all aspects of our "self." Our free will may be depraved through false reasoning or through choosing unrestrained freedom and an inclination to content the senses. When our free will turns from understanding and reason, there is nothing we can do but do what it wants in agreement with the external senses. According to traditional psychology it is almost impossible to retrieve a perverted will.

FREE-WILL ALLIES WITH IMAGINATION AGAINST REASON

Our imagination is likely to become an enemy of our ability to reason. As our sense of imagination is near the outer or external senses (seeing, hearing, tasting, touching and smelling), it may seduce us to accept something and then, as an intermediary between our external senses and our animal soul (lust and anger, affective-behavioral systems), establish a coalition against our ability to reason. This could explain how rash judgments are strengthened in our imagination arousing our animal soul (affective-behavioral systems), and over-throwing our ability to reason. Our imagination can be a dangerous guide to us in terms of our ability to center our "self."

FREE-WILL ALLIES WITH IMAGINATION
AND THE EXTERNAL SENSES AGAINST REASON

Our knowledge, it will be recalled, is dependent upon our external senses because they are the doors through which all impressions from the outer world pass to our higher functions of thought and they may also dominate over our ability to reason. The ready response of our ability to reason the reports from the outer or external senses by-pass our conscience as they quickly turn to a new stimulus. The external senses are easily moved by the animal soul (affective-behavioral systems). A picture or mere description is enough to awaken passions of love or grief.

The strength of our sense impressions as opposed to our ability to reason can be recalled when we reflect on the parting of two friends. The idea of some particular gesture in a parting friend strikes us more deeply than all the reasoning in the world. The sound of a name repeated, certain words or a sad tone go to our very heart. A present object moves our animal soul (affective-behavioral system) much more vehemently than when we perceive an image through our recall. When the desired thing is not present, our imagination represents the pleasure as far off, but when the thing desired is present, nothing seems to be left but to attain it.

Our external senses are capable of a degree of knowledge and of pleasure and pain. Since they cannot comprehend the full meaning of objects presented to them, they report to us merely outward images and in their impressions emphasize qualities agreeable to our external senses rather than to our general welfare. Not knowing all that takes place in imagination and in reason, the external senses may accept enemies as friends. Through their strength, they may provoke serious disturbances in us.

They work on our imagination without waiting for our reasoning to deliberate; they set off an alarm to our animal soul (affective-behavioral systems) to the extent that the voice of our reason cannot be heard nor the advice of understanding be accepted by our free will. Representing pleasures that are most apparent and present, they strongly provoke our animal soul. Even though they are our first teacher, instead of freeing us from deceit, they are seen to be able to deceive us themselves.

FREE-WILL ALLIES WITH IMAGINATION IN THE AFFECTIVE-BEHAVIORAL SYSTEMS (ANIMAL SOUL) AGAINST REASON

Our animal soul (affective-behavioral systems) is naturally disposed to allow us to regulate it through our ability to reason. When it joins in an alliance with our free will, our animal soul and free will follow the external senses. Our outer or external senses respond to an object. Our reason deliberates. Our free will is naturally disposed towards the positive as is our reason. However, when our free will is under the influence of our animal soul (affective-behavioral systems), our free will only sees the present which fills our imagination more readily than does the future and our reason is subdued.

Our free-will is a superior function to our animal soul (affective-behavioral systems). It is joined with our reason in the same way our animal soul (affective-behavioral systems) is joined to our imagination. We are naturally disposed to guide our free will towards action which is for our well-being.

However, we contain an inferior kind of thought-action process and that is the process of imagination-animal soul (affective-behavioral systems). Both of the latter (imagination and affective-behavior) act rashly without the deliberation of our reason. They are often too powerful to allow our reason to advise and our free will to accept the advice.

Our will is easily misled. Naturally inclined to avoid conflict, it succumbs to our animal soul (affective-behavioral systems). They all grow out of our system of motivation and so have an established relationship. Our reason can control our action only through our free will and our free will frequently yields to our animal soul (affective-behavioral systems). Strife within us is most often between our reason and our systems arising out of motivation. Our external senses entice our imagination and our imagination joins with the animal soul (affective-behavioral systems) and they, in turn, entice our free will away from following our reason.

CENTERING THROUGH FREE-WILL

As nature in its mode of operation was perfected by the Creator in us with the gift of consciousness, by-passing our free will causes an imbalance in our natural harmony and equilibrium. This is because the process of our free will within us needs to consciously seek the counsel of reason as the regulator of nature within us. When our regulator is by-passed, our system loses its balance and equilibrium. If our nurturing process has not been able to preserve a healthy, moral self, traditional psychology provides the means to restore health.

If our free will accepts the guidance of our reason, we can become centered (as long as our reason remains balanced as well). The ideas upon which our internal sense of reason deliberates come from our imagination. Our internal sense of imag-

ination may be functioning according to the Divine Will, operating through universal and particular guidance. This process
becomes strong when good habits are formed in us from birth.

Without this, we become prone to negative traits and our
free will is not inclined towards choosing positive traits or attitudes. It is motivated by our natural disposition of attraction
to pleasure, the original goal of which is to preserve the
species. However, when it is unregulated, even our species is
threatened by over, under or un-developed eating, sex, drinking, and so forth. Our mirror of self is so encrusted with rust
and dust that we no longer can see our "self." We become
alienated from our natural disposition and lose all sense of
identity and direction. We readily then forget our original goal
of submission to the Will of God by completing the perfection
of nature in its mode of operation, that is, becoming conscious
of our "self." We are no longer able to avoid pain/harm because
the natural disposition of even our immunity systems break
down. Our free-will, naturally disposed to be free to choose or
not to choose to submit to the Will of God, is no longer free but
enslaved by our animal soul (affective and behavioral systems) leading to the tyranny of our "self" in complete opposition to the original natural disposition of our free will to being
just.

Al-Ghazzali recognizes the human will to control everything, but points out that lacking the power to do so, we seek
knowledge of everything in order to gain mastery.

> There is this in the nature of a human being
> that requires him to desire he be everything. Since
> he is incapable of this, he desires that everything be
> his; that is, that everything be subservient to him
> and under his control and (subject to) his will.
> However, he is incapable of achieving this also, for
> there are two kinds of existing things: One kind is
> that which the control of man does not touch, such

as the heavens, stars, the substances of the angels and the devils, and that which is beneath the earth, at the depths of the oceans, and under mountains. Therefore, man desires to conquer all of these through knowledge so that they come under the control of his knowledge, even though they are not in his power. For this reason he desires that the kingdoms of heaven and earth, the wonders of the land and sea, all be made known, just as a person who is incapable of arranging the chess pieces, but wishes in all events to know how they have been placed, for this too is a kind of mastery.[37]

And once we are winning the battle with our animal soul (lust and anger) and our satanic aspect (ego, imagination), we have "cleared our heart of the thorns of worldly temptation," al-Ghazzali speaks of the seeds of good character that will be able to grow.

So, when the heart has been cleared of the thorns of worldly temptations and the seeds have been planted, nothing still remains that is related to free choice; it has chosen to be there (in that condition). After that, one remains waiting for what will grow and appear. Usually the seed is not wasted, for God Most High says: *Whoever desires the harvest of the Hereafter, We give him increase in his harvest.* (Q. 42:20) He says: "Whoever cultivates the work of the Hereafter and sows the seed, We shall bestow increase upon him.". . . .[38]

5 For the beasts of burden, their nutriment and their happiness is in eating, sleeping, and copulating. If you are of their kind, you try to satisfy your stomach and your genitals night and day. As for predatory beasts, their nutriment and their happiness is in giving free rein to tearing apart, killing, and rage. The nutri-

ment of satanic forces is the encouragement of evil, treachery, and deceit. If you are of them, get busy in their activities and attain your ease and good fortune!

The intention in attaining good character, according to al-Ghazzali, is to develop angelic qualities to replace the satanic.

> Know that the (spiritual) happiness of a human being is that one becomes of the nature of angels; for one's essence is of them and one has come into this world a stranger. One's source is the world of the angels. Every foreign characteristic that one bears from here distances one from being in conformity with (the angels). When going to that place, one must become of their character and not carry any attributes from this place.[39]

The Quran gives references to what having a good character means:

> Know that the signs of a good character are those which God Most High has described concerning the believers in the Quran in the first ten verses of the chapter beginning: *Successful indeed are the believers*, (Q. 23:1-10) and in the verse where He says: *Those who turn in repentance and those who serve (Him) . . .*, (Q. 9:112) and in those verses where He says: *And the servants of the Compassionate are they who walk upon the earth modestly to the end* (of the chapter). (Q. 25:63-77)[40]

Even with angelic qualities one needs to keep to moderation in order to complete and perfect human nature according to al-Ghazzali:

> In the same manner, all character has two aspects: one is praiseworthy and one is blamewor-

thy. The objective is moderation. For example, we order the miser to give away wealth until it becomes easy for him, but not to the point of extravagance; for that is also blameworthy. But the scale for (weighing) that is from the Religious Law, just as the scale for (weighing) the treatment of the body is the science of medicine. He must become so that whatever the Law commands him to give, he gives, and its giving becomes easy for him and that there not be in him a demand to keep and hold on to (wealth). And whatever the Religious Law commands him to keep, he should keep and the urge to give (of that) not be in him so that he be moderate. Therefore, if those impulses continue to appear in him—but he represses them by force—he is still ill; however, he is praiseworthy because he is indeed forcing himself to take his medicine and this compulsion is the way that (good character) will become natural to him.[41]

Again al-Ghazzali stresses moderation.

Any attribute which it is not possible for a person to eliminate, should be kept at the (the level of) moderation so that in one way it is as though it were eliminated. As water is not devoid of warmth or coldness, that which is tepid and equable resembles that which is devoid of both (extremes). Therefore, moderation and the mean in all qualities have been commanded because they are better.[42]

Our angelic hosts of conscience and will power have to struggle against our animal soul. What fuel did God give for the armaments of the battle? What is the source of energy?

According to traditional psychology, energy in our liver undergoes successive processes of sublimation in our heart and brain. The purity of this energy and according to the function it performs as natural, vital, or nervous energy, serves a group of powers of nature in its mode of operation.

Vegetal functions promote nutrition, growth, and reproduction. The nutritive function works by a number of subordinate systems: retention, digestion, assimilation, expulsion. The energy for the vegetal functions originates in our liver where our humors are, as well so well known today to Chinese, Indian and ancient Greek methods of alternative medicine.

Our humors move by natural energy through the veins carrying sustenance to the body, performing the tasks of the vegetal systems. According to traditionalists like Ibn Sina (Avicenna) we contain four humors:

> Humor (*akhlat*) or body-fluid is that fluid, moist, physical substance into which our aliment is transformed. That part of the aliment which has the capacity to be transformed into body substance, either by itself or in combination with something else thereby being capable of assimilation by the members or organs, and completely integrated into the tissues, is the healthy or good humor. It is what replaces the loss which the body substance undergoes.
>
> Primary fluids are the sanguineous humor (blood), the serous humor (phlegm), the bilious humor (yellow bile) and the atrabilious humor (black bile).[43]

THE SANGUINEOUS HUMOR

> The nature [dynamic aspect] of the sanguineous humor is hot and moist in temperament. It may be normal or abnormal, conforming to its nature or not. Normal blood is red in color, sweet in taste and free from smell.[44]

THE SEROUS HUMOR

> The nature of the serous humor is cold and

moist in temperament. It may be normal or abnormal. Normal (sweet) serous humor can be transformed into blood at any time as it is an imperfectly matured blood. It is a kind of sweet fluid which is only slightly colder than the body, but it is much colder than the bilious and blood humors.[45]

THE BILIOUS HUMOR

The bilious humor is the foam of blood. It is bright in color. It is light and pungent. The more red, it is, the hotter it is. It is formed in the liver and then follows one of two courses: either it circulates with the blood or it passes on to the gall-bladder. The part which passes into the blood stream assists in two purposes. First of all, the portion which goes to the blood is essential for nutrition of organs like the lungs. It makes the blood light and thin for easy passage through the narrow channels of the body. The portion which goes into the gallbladder is thus prevented, from vitiating the body and providing nutrition to the gallbladder. Its subsidiary functions are the cleansing of the intestine from the thick and viscid mucus and stimulation of the musculature of the intestine and rectum for proper defecation.[46]

THE ATRABILIOUS HUMOR

Atrabilious humor is cold and dry in nature. There are a natural and abnormal varieties.

Normal atrabilious humor is a sediment of the normal blood. It has a taste between sweetness and bitterness. After being formed in the liver, a part goes to the blood and another to the spleen.

The part which goes with the blood is essential for two purposes: the nutrition of organs such as the bones which have an appreciable quantity of the atrabilious bile in their composition, and to make the blood properly thick and heavy.

The portion which is in excess of these require-
ments is taken up by the spleen essentially for its
own nutrition but also to save the blood from being
damaged. The portion which goes from the spleen
into the stomach serves the purpose of making the
stomach strong and firm. It also stimulates the
appetite by its sour taste.

This action of atrabilious humor is somewhat
similar to that of the bilious humor. Just as the surplus of bile in the blood goes to the gallbladder, and
the surplus from the gallbladder passes into the
intestine, the excess of atrabilious humor from the
blood goes to the spleen, what is left over from the
spleen goes to the stomach to induce appetite. The
surplus of bilious humor excites peristaltic movements and thus assists evacuation, but the surplus
of atrabilious humor encourages the intake of food.
So, blessed be God, the best of creators and the
mightiest of rulers![47]

VITAL ENERGY OF THE HEART

Natural energy of the vegetal functions arises from blood
in the liver. It passes with the humors through the veins to all
parts of the body. Some natural energy and humors enter the
cavity of the heart and through transformation there, becomes
the vital energy, a substance less gross than that from the
liver. Vital energies are carried to the organs of the body by
our arteries. They make life possible. Vital energies are transformed in the brain where they become nervous energy. This
makes perception and motivation to movement possible.

Vital energy of the sensitive functions arise from blood in
the heart as transformed natural energy and move by way of
the body through the arteries. The heart is the seat of life, of
heat, of pulse, of the vital energies, and of nature in its mode
of operation. It is the organ which lives first and dies last.

Cognitive Vital and Nervous Energies Respond to Natural Dispositions

Nervous energy arises in the brain from the vital energy reaching it from the heart. The brain is the center for motivation and perception. Motivation allows movement and perception consists of external and internal senses.

We have no control over these energies and how they are sent throughout the body except through what we eat and the air that we breath. However, we can choose to become aware of our "self," in which case we would be forcing our "nervous energy" to be used for this purpose. This will serve to arm our angelic energies.

Awakening the Natural Disposition to Consciousness of Self

Consciousness is developed through "reminders" or Signs that remind the self of its origin and of the nobility it gained when it received the infusion of the Divine Spirit, signified by human values. They include the knowledge that God is One, that truth, beauty, goodness, and love exist and are expressed in the original creation we try to imitate in response to a natural disposition to creativity, imitating the Original Creation.

Nothing happens without a source of energy. The more energy we have, the more vibrancy we have. While it is usually thought that if we eat better food, we will have more energy and this is true to some extent, there is also a qualitative energy that comes from spiritual practices which cannot be measured in the usual sense. Its presence can only be known through the resulting actions.

6 As for the angels, their nutriment and their happiness is the contemplation of the Divine Presence.

They are immune from the lust, anger and the attributes of the beasts and predators. If you have the angelic essence in your nature, strive to come to know the Divine Presence and open yourself to the contemplation of Its Beauty. Liberate yourself from the grip of lust and anger. Strive until you understand the reason for the creation of these bestial traits within you. Were they created to capture you, to carry you into service of the self, and to enslave you in forced labor day and night? You must capture them before they capture you! You (must) make of one your vehicle and of the other your weapon for the journey that has been put before you. Use them in these few days that we are in this stopping place to hunt, with their aid, the seed of your own (spiritual) happiness.

We are generated out of the Divine Spirit and natural dispositions or "soul" of the mineral, plant, and animal forms, which have been guided by universal guidance. We may evolve the ability of consciousness through particular guidance if we will to do so. This enhances the actualization of conscience and will power as our own special natural disposition. Al-Ghazzali points out:

> Know that a human being has been created of two things: one is the body which can be seen with the physical eye. The other is the spirit which cannot be perceived except by the eye of the heart. For each one of these two there is goodness and unseemliness. One is called the beauty of creation; the other, the beauty of disposition. Beauty of disposition consists of the inner form, just as beauty of creation consists of the outer form. As the outer form is not good if only the eyes are good, or only the mouth is good, or only the nose is good, so that the eyes, mouth, and nose together are not good and

not suited to one another; in the same way the inner form is not good so long as four powers or faculties in it are not good: the power of reason, the power of anger, the power of lust, and the power of preserving fairness and balance among the other three.

As for the power of reason, by that we mean wisdom; the goodness of which is enough to easily distinguish between truth and lies in speech, (between) the good and the unseemly in deeds, and between the true and the false in principles of belief. When this perfection has been achieved by the heart, it is from that which wisdom comes into being: the source of all kinds of happiness, as God Most High said: *And he unto whom wisdom is given, he hath truly received abundant good.* (Q. 2:269)

The goodness of the power of anger is that it be under the command of reason and the Law and arise at their command and end at their command.

The goodness of the power of the carnal appetite or lust is that it not be rebellious and that it be under the command of the Religious Law and reason so that its obedience to them may be easy for it.

The goodness of the power of justice is that it keep anger and lust subjugated to the direction of religion and reason.[48]

Dispositions or states of being are both natural and acquired. Whether natural or acquired, either can be regulated by conscious or unconscious habits, habits being the continual repetition of certain acts.

Natural dispositions are never changed, in the sense that the original is lost, but rather, through nurturing, they can become hidden or concealed just as a mirror can lose its reflective capacity with the formation of rust, dust, or fog. The mirror is still there, but it reflects rust, dust, and fog rather than the its original, naturally disposed polished surface. Therefore, the natural disposition changes at the same time that it is always there and no energy is lost in the change. Al-Ghazzali explains further:

> Know that God Most High has praised Mustafa (☫) for his good disposition, saying: *And, lo! Thou art of a tremendous nature!* (Q. 68:4) And the Messenger (☫) said: "I was sent to complete the excellences of character." And he (☫) said: "The greatest thing placed in the scales is a good disposition."
>
> Someone appeared before the Messenger (☫) and asked: "What is religion (*din*)?" He answered: "A good disposition." They came from the right and the left, asking (the same question again and again). He replied in the same way until at the last time he said: "Do you not know?—that you not anger." He (☫) was asked: "What is the most virtuous of actions?" He said: "A good disposition."
>
> Someone said to the Messenger (☫): "Give me some advice." He said: "Fear God Most High wherever you may be." (The man) said: "Another." He said: "Do a good deed after every bad act in order to erase it." (The man) said: "Another." He said: "Mix with people good-naturedly." And he (☫) said: "God Most High will not make whomever He has given a good disposition and a good appearance the food of fire."
>
> And he (☫) was told: " Such-and-such a woman fasts by day and spends her night in formal prayer, but has a bad disposition and her tongue afflicts her neighbors." He said: "Her place is in hell." And the Messenger (☫) said: "A bad disposition ruins devotion as vinegar (ruins) honey."
>
> And the Messenger (☫) used to say as he made supplication: "O Lord God! Thou hast created my creation well; make my disposition also good." And

> he (ﷺ) used to say: "O Lord God! Grant (us) health,
> vigor, and a good disposition." The Messenger (ﷺ)
> was asked: "What is the best thing that God Most
> High gives His servant?" He answered: "A good dis-
> position." And he (ﷺ) said: "A good disposition
> destroys sins as the sun (destroys) ice."[49]

We are born with a natural disposition to meet physiolog-
ical and psychological needs of the self. Psychological needs,
which are part of the our natural disposition, are positive
aspects of nature in its mode of operation trying to perfect our
"self." These form the mirror of our "self." The nurturing
process clouds, distorts, and darkens this mirror, thereby distancing us from our true nature. Change is effected through
methods known as "polishing" or "purifying" the mirror of self
so that it can once again reflect the positive aspects of our
nature which we were naturally disposed by God (*fitrat*). Al-
Ghazzali clarifies:

> . . . . Just as with outward beauty where extreme
> goodness and extreme unseemliness are not com-
> mon and most fall in between, so it is with a good
> disposition. Therefore, every one must make an
> effort so that, even if one does not achieve perfec-
> tion, one comes nearer to the degree of perfection. If
> all of one's character is not good; well, some parts or
> more of it will be good. As there is not limit to the
> differences between beauty and ugliness, the same
> is true of one's character.
>   This is the whole meaning of a good disposition.
> It is not one thing, nor ten, nor a hundred; for it is
> much more. However, it originates with the powers
> of wisdom, anger (courage), lust (temperance), and
> justice: the rest are branches of it.[50]

Change, growth, and transformation in the traditional
perspective do not mean that the natural disposition of repro-

duction or self-preservation should be repressed or suppressed because the human race could not exist without them. The point made in the traditions is that the mean and moderation, balance and equilibrium, are the norm so that all natural dispositions function properly.

Dispositions are described as "that which is the source of all of the actions that the self undertakes spontaneously without thinking about them." A natural disposition may be the result of natural and physical make-up by which we are endowed at birth with what is known physiologically as temperament. Temperament arises from the combination of elemental qualities of hot-wet, hot-dry, cold-wet, and cold-dry which develop depending on the constellation of birth, the geographic location of our parents at the time of the intercourse which leads to conception, of a mother during the time of pregnancy, the food that they eat, and the air that they breath. Even though temperament is natural, it can be changed, regulated, or neutralized as a disposition or psychological structure through moral healing and the centering process.

ATTITUDE: POSITIVE AND NEGATIVE

A disposition that becomes embedded in the self is known as a trait or an attitude. In the traditional perspective we are created pure and good and start life with a "clean slate," in the sense that we are free of negative traits and attitudes. Negative traits develop through contact with one's environment—parents, family, friends, schooling, work, and so forth. These traits are directly related to the way a person lives and thinks and are reinforced by one's words and deeds and concealed if negative resulting from the lack of nurturing guidance. Penetrating through our "self," traits or attitudes become the origin and cause of human actions.

When a negative disposition is reinforced through behavior, it becomes imbedded in us as a trait which requires greater conscious effort on the part of our cognitive system to undo. Al-Ghazzali describes our positive and negative traits:

> The power of anger, should it become excessive, is called recklessness; while if it is deficient, it is called cowardice and spiritlessness. When it is in balance—not too much or too little—it is called courage. Courage gives rise to nobility, high-mindedness, bravery, mildness, patience, moderation, control of (inappropriate) anger, and characteristics like these. From recklessness come boasting, vanity, conceit, impetuosity, vain-glory, throwing oneself into dangerous affairs, and the like. From its deficiency come self-abasement, helplessness, anxiety, fawning, and abjectness.
>
> The power of lust, should it become excessive, is called gluttony. From it arise impudence, foulness, unmanliness, uncleanliness, jealousy, being despised by the powerful, being contemptuous of the poor, love of this world and the like. If it is deficient, lethargy, dastardliness, and dishonor (come). When it is in balance, it is called temperance; from it come modesty, contentment, patience, tolerance, grace, wit, and approval.
>
> Each one of these has two extremes which are condemned and unseemly, but the medium is good and praiseworthy. That medium, between those two extremes, is narrower than a hair. That medium is its Straight Path. It is as narrow as the Bridge of the Hereafter. Whoever walks straight upon this bridge, is sure to (cross) that (other) Bridge tomorrow (in safety).[51]

The purpose of traditional psychology, then, is to first try to preserve the *fitrat* or natural dispositions of our self—which is called the healthy self— through the nurturing process.

One of the methods of both preservation of one's natural disposition or restoration back to it is self-training and conscious effort to adopt positive habits. It has been shown through centuries of experience that this will lead to a positive disposition and the stabilization of positive traits resulting in a healthy self. Traditional psychology and the methods of preservation of psychic health and/or its restoration when an imbalance occurs, basically deal with the development of traits that are slow to decline. We become centered when traits fall under the regulation of reason so that a positive disposition evolves.

The positive traits that indicate "centeredness" in traditional psychology develop out of the previous three systems: affective, behavioral, and cognitive. The positive disposition of the affective system is temperance. The positive disposition of the behavioral system is courage. The positive disposition of the cognitive intellect is wisdom. When these three positive dispositions are in balance, regulated by the conscious cognitive system, the fourth positive disposition is attained, that of justice. According to traditional psychology, fairness or justice is one of the natural dispostions of our free will. These are the positive traits all of which appear in the Quran and the *sunnah*. They are chosen as the "mothers of character" from among the many positive traits mentioned because of the central role they play in the analysis of our "self." They are distinguished by various functions therein. These four positive traits are also mentioned by Plato and Aristotle with a slight difference in values. They are accepted into the Islamic tradition by al-Ghazzali for two clear reasons: first of all, they are part of the Quran and the *sunnah*; and secondly they can be arrived at through the observation of nature.

Therefore, these positive traits are part of the Signs of guidance and can be acquired by accepting particular guidance.

Al-Ghazzali operationalizes the positive traits:

The goodness of the power of anger is that it be under the command of wisdom and the Law and arise at their command and end at their command.

The goodness of the power of lust is that it not be rebellious and that it be under the command of the Religious Law and reason so that its obedience to them may be easy for it.

The goodness of the power of justice is that it keep anger and lust subjugated to the direction of religion and reason.

The power of wisdom, should it become excessive and involved in bad works, gives rise to deception and hypocrisy; while if it is deficient, it gives rise to foolishness and ignorance. However, when it is in balance, it gives rise to good planning, correct opinion, right thinking, and sound insight.[52]

THE QURAN AND CENTERING THROUGH THE POSITIVE TRAITS

The Quran mentions these traits which bring about "centeredness" when they work together in balance and harmony giving equilibrium to the self. All four are referred to in one verse:

"Believers are those who believe in God and His Messenger then they doubt not," a belief that is a consequence of reason and consciousness as the highest form of wisdom, *"and strive with their benefits in the Way of God,"* indicating temperance since this striving is only possible to be in the Way of God (nature/nurture or takwini/ tashrii guidance) when the unconscious, affective/ emotive function is regulated by the rational, conscious belief in God and His Messenger, *"and strive with their lives in the Way of God,"* clearly referring to the behavioral function and courage since this positive trait is only possible of attainment in the Way of God when the preconscious, behavioral function is regulated by the rational, conscious

belief in God and His Messenger; *"they are the truthful ones, "* the just. (Q. 49:15)

Each of the three positive traits: courage, temperance, and wisdom may develop as negative traits through an overdevelopment, or underdevelopment of one of the three functions of affect, behavior, or cognition.

Al-Ghazzali counsels moderation and balance as previously mentioned:

> It is for this that God Most High has ordained the middle way in all characteristics. He has forbidden both extremes, and gives punishment (for them), saying: *And those who, when they spend, are neither prodigal nor grudging; and there is a firm station between the two.* (Q. 25:67) He praised the person who does not skimp in spending and is not extravagant, but stands between the two. And the Messenger (ﷺ) was told (by God): *And let not thy hand be chained to thy neck, nor open it with a complete opening, lest thou sit down rebuked, denuded.* (Q. 17:29) He said: "Do not tie up your hand so as to give nothing, nor open it completely at one time and give away everything lest you be left without provisions and helpless.
>
> So then, know that the absolutely good disposition is that in which all elements are balanced and correct within it, just as a beautiful countenance is that in which all of its parts are right and good.[53]

And recommends methods of treatment:

> Know that for whoever desires to expel his bad disposition from himself there is only one way, and that is that he do the opposite of whatever that (bad) disposition commands him (to do). Lust or carnal appetite cannot be broken except by opposition. Everything is overcome by its contrary, just as the

treatment of an illness which causes heat is the eating of cold (foods). The treatment of every illness
which arises from anger is patience. The treatment
of whatever arises from arrogance is humility. The
treatment of whatever arises from miserliness is
giving away wealth. The same (rule) is valid for all.

(1) There are some which are not affected by
human choice, just as a one cannot grow an apple
tree from the stone of a date; but one can grow a
date palm with the nurture and care that it the
requires. In the same way, the roots of anger and
lust cannot be driven out of a human being.
However, anger and lust can be brought to the limit
of moderation with discipline. This is made plain
with experience.

(2) However, with respect to some people is its
more difficult. This difficulty is for two reasons: one
is that it has become stronger in the essence of one's
innate nature; the second is that one has been in
obedience to it for a long time, to the point that one
is mastered by it.[54]

**7 When you have obtained that seed of happiness,
place those (those tools) underfoot and turn your face
to the resting place of your own (spiritual) happiness,
that resting place for which the elite expression is the
Divine Presence and for which the common expression
is "Paradise."**

There are those who never seek spiritual happiness. Al-
Ghazzali gives reasons why:

> Know that the reason for someone's not reach-
> ing God is that he has not traveled the path. The
> reason for someone's not traveling the path is that
> he has not sought it. The reason for someone's not
> seeking it is the he did not know, and his belief was

incomplete. Indeed, the desire for the quest for the provisions of the Hereafter appears in whoever knows that the world causes misery and is but of a few days in duration, while the Hereafter is pure and everlasting. It is not a hardship for him to exchange something despicable for something valuable. Putting down the earthen jug so that tomorrow one will receive a golden jug is not very difficult.

He describes those who seek spiritual happiness:

> . . . . if the desire for God Most High appears in someone, and he is one of those about whom God Most High says: *And he who desires the Hereafter. . . .* (Q. 17:19) He should know what the effort and striving is required. God continues: . . . *and strives for it with the effort necessary.* (Q. 17:19) Know that this effort is traveling the way! The traveler must first possess certain requisites which he has previously accomplished; then there is the document that he must hold firmly; then there is a fortress and a castle which will give him refuge.[56]

One attains to the Divine Presence by undertaking the greater struggle. Al-Ghazzali quotes the famous saying of the Prophet:

> The Messenger (ﷺ) used to say to the Companions when they returned from battle in defense of religion: "Ye have come from the lesser struggle to the greater struggle." They asked: "What is that?" He answered: "The striving against one's animal soul (*jihad-i nafs*)." And the Messenger (ﷺ) said: "Restrain the torment of yourself from the animal soul and do give rein to its whims in disobedience to God Most High Who will judge you tomorrow and curse you until your parts all curse one another."[57]

According to the Prophet as quoted by al-Ghazzali in the *Alchemy,* the heart of all acts is our intention. It is for this that the Messenger (ﷺ) said: "God Most High does not look at your outward appearance and qualities; He looks at you heart and deeds." (His) looking at the heart is because it is the locus of intention. And the Messenger (ﷺ) said: "Acts are according to intention." Every person receives from his act of worship that which is his intention for that.[58]

> Know that the learned have said: 'First learn the intention of the act, then, the act.' Someone said: 'Teach me an act that I may be engaged with night and day so that I not be devoid of good at any time.' They said: 'If you cannot perform a good deed, then continually form good intentions so that the spiritual reward of that (unperformed deed) be obtained.[59]

Our intention, according to a Tradition of the Prophet is better than our deed. Al-Ghazzali explains what this means.

> Know that the Messenger (ﷺ) has said: "The intention of the believer is better than his deed." The intention of the believer is better than his deed: he did not mean by this that an intention without the deed is better than a deed without the intention; for this itself is not a secret that a deed without the intention is not an act of worship, whilst an intention without the deed is an act of worship. Instead, the meaning is that one's devotion is with body and heart, and these are two parts. Of these two, that which is in the heart is better. The reason for this is that object of the act of the body is to alter the nature of the heart. The object of the intention and the act of the heart is not that it alter the nature of the body.
> People imagine thus, that an intention is nec-

essary for an act, but the truth of the matter is that the act must be for the intention because the purpose of an act is to cause the heart to turn toward the next world. It is the traveler to the next world. (Eternal) happiness or misfortune will be its portion.[60]

Intention needs to precede every act in order to have possible spiritual rewards. Without the intention, it is recorded— as good or bad depending on what the intention is—but without spiritual reward according to al-Ghazzali:

> Know that there are three kinds of deeds: acts of devotion, sins, and the permitted.
> (1) (The first kind: Sins.) It may that because the Messenger (ﷺ) said: "Verily acts are based on one's intentions," that a sin, with a good intention, can also be counted as an act of worship. This is wrong. This kind of intention has no effect, but a bad intention makes it worse. It is like this: a person backbites in order to please someone; or he establishes a mosque, school, or retreat using unlawful wealth and says: "My intention was good." He does not know even this much: that it is not good because a resolution to do good with evil is another evil. If he understands all (of this), he is a sinner. If he does not know and imagines that this is good, he is also a sinner, for acquiring knowledge is a religious obligation. Most of mankind's perdition is from ignorance."
> (2) The second kind: Acts of Devotion. In these, intention has two aspects with regard to effect: one is that its basis becomes correct with the intention; and the other is that however much the intention is increased, the spiritual reward is multiplied. Whoever acquires the knowledge (of making an) intention can make ten good intentions with one act of devotion so that it becomes several acts of devo-

tion. For example when one goes into retreat in the mosque."

(3) The third kind is the permitted. Let no rational being who wallows in the permitted like heedless beasts neglect a good intention. It is a great loss. He will be questioned about all of (these acts) and there will be a reckoning concerning all of the permitted things. He will be held accountable if his intention is bad; and if it is good, it will reflect on him; otherwise, it will be quits. But he will have wasted time and spent in that in which there is no benefit for him, and he will have disobeyed this verse: *And forget not thy portion of the world and be thou kind even as God has been kind to thee.* (Q. 28:77) That is, the world is transitory; take your portion from it so that it stays with you. The Messenger (☙) said: "The servant of God will be asked about all that he has done, even to the amount of collyrium applied about the eyes, or the bit of earth rubbed with between fingers, or the hand placed upon the clothing of a brother.[61]

For anyone of us overcome by passion al-Ghazzali says the best way to discipline it is through undertaking the greater struggle.

Whoever is overcome by passion, that passion is one's object of worship. When this state becomes (one's) true nature, one must uncover or discover it through the greater struggle, not through argument.[62]

8 All of these matters must be learned so that you may know a little about yourself. The prize of the Way of Religion (*al-din*) for whoever does not come to know these is like husks, and he is deprived of the true nature [and the best part] of Religion.

As mentioned before, *al-din* can be translated as "tradition" (not to be confused with the sayings and actions of the Prophet which are Tradition (*hadith*) with a captial T).

Al-Ghazzali uses the concept of the spiritual heart sometimes to mean "mind" and sometimes "emotion." Its meaning depends upon the context. He discusses it using his three fundamentals: knowledge, states and acts.

KNOWLEDGE: THE HEART

The spiritual heart al-Ghazzali points out has to be turned away from this world to the next.

> The turning about of the heart itself is not more than one thing: that it turn from this world to the Hereafter; rather, to turn from this world to God Most High. The direction of the heart does not precede desire and will power or inclination. When the desire for this world gains mastery over the heart, it turns to this world. Its attachment to this world is a desire that has been with it from the beginning of creation. When the wishes of God Most High and of seeing the Hereafter dominate, its nature changes and it turns toward another direction.[63]

The soundness of the heart according to al-Ghazzali is in its beings the loving friend of our innate nature.

> Know that just as the soundness of the body, hands, feet, and eyes lies in that each one of them is able to do completely that for which it was created—so that the eye sees well and the foot walks well—so the soundness of the heart lies in that its special quality that is part of its original innate nature and the reason for which it was created. It is to be the loving friend of that which is the basis of

our original innate nature and this should be easy
for the heart.[64]

Knowledge is acquired through our spiritual heart (mind).
The spiritual heart is the seat of the Intellect, source of faith
and object of God's sight. Reference to the "spiritual" heart in
the Quran and sunnah refers to that aspect of "self" which
comes to know the meaning or nature of things as al-Ghazzali
points out:

> So, that amount of power is useful which is the
> means of acquiring knowledge. Knowledge is
> (acquired) by the application of the heart, not the
> body; and the heart endures and is everlasting.
> When a savant departs from this world, the knowl-
> edge remains (with him). That knowledge is his
> light by which he sees the Divine Presence so as to
> obtain the pleasure (in comparison) to which all of
> the other pleasures of Paradise fall short.
> Knowledge has no dependency upon anything that
> will be voided at death, for neither wealth nor the
> hearts of people are attached to knowledge; rather,
> it is the essence of God Most High, His attributes,
> His wisdom in the dominion and kingdom; and the
> wonders of the probabilities in the possible, the nec-
> essary, and the impossible; for they are timeless
> and eternal. They never change because the neces-
> sary never becomes impossible, nor the impossible
> possible. However, knowledge which is connected
> with created transitory things has no weight, such
> as the knowledge of language, for example; for lan-
> guage is created and transitory, its weight is that it
> is the means of knowing the Book and the practice
> (of the Prophet). Knowing the Book and the practice
> is knowing God Most High and the cutting away of
> the obstacles on the path to Him.[65]

STATES: THE HEART

. . . . the heart has been so created that when an inclination or desire appears in it, when the body rises in agreement with that, that quality becomes more firmly and strongly established in the heart. For example, when mercy for the orphan appears in the heart, if the hand is placed upon (the orphan's) head, that mercy grows stronger and the awareness of the heart increases. When the import of humility appears, one acts humbly with the head too and it approaches the ground. The intention of all acts of worship and the desire for the good is not that one turn to the world, but to the Hereafter.[66]

. . . .. God Most High is the nourishment of the heart, just as food is the nourishment of the body. A body from which the craving for food has departed or in which it has grown weak is sick. A heart from which the love for God Most High has departed or in which it has grown weak is sick. It is for this that God Most High said: *Say: If your fathers and your sons. . .* (Q. 9:24) [67]

Al-Ghazzali says that the defects of the heart can be recognized in four ways:

(1) One is that one resort to an experienced and mature spiritual guide so that that spiritual guide may examine him and disclose the person's defects to him. In this era, this is unusual and rare.

(2) The second is that one have a sympathetic friend watch over oneself, one who will not conceal one's defects out of flattery nor magnify them out of envy. This too is rare. Dawud Tayi, may God have mercy upon him, was asked: "Why do you not associate and mix with people?" He replied: "What is the point of associating with a people who see my faults and conceal them from me?"

(3) The third is that one listen to the talk of one's enemies about oneself, for the eye of the enemy always falls upon faults. Even if he exaggerates out of his enmity, his words are still not devoid of truth.

(4) The fourth is that one should study people. One should constantly be on the watch for any defect in oneself that one sees in someone else. One should suspect one's self, for it may be the same.[68]

ACTIONS: HEART

Thus, the aim of all acts is to turn the heart. The aim of prostration is not that the forehead move from the air to touch the ground; rather, it is that the heart turn from desires and arrogance to humility. The purpose of (uttering) God is greater is not that the tongue twist and flick about; rather, it is that the heart turn from glorification of the ego (animal soul) to the glorification of God Most High. The purpose of casting stones during the greater pilgrimage is not to increase the number of stones at a particular spot or to exercise the arm; rather, is that the heart stand firm upon its servitude (of God) and abandon the pursuit of carnal desires and the control of one's own reason, and become obedient to (God's) command. One removes the reins from his own hand and surrenders them to the hand of (God's) command. As he says: "At Thy service, in proof of Truth, in worship and as a slave." The purpose of the sacrifice is not that a sheep be killed; rather, it is that the foulness of miserliness depart from your breast; you do not have compassion for animals because of your nature, but you have it because of the command (of God). When it is said: "Slaughter this sheep!" you do not say: "What has this wretch done? Why should I punish it?" Rather you abandon yourself and in truth become non-existent; for the servant (of God) is non-existent with respect to God and he is truly intoxicated

with God. All acts of worship are like this. . . .[69]
Acts (performed) with that intention become established and confirmed. Consequently, the act is for
the confirmation of the desire and the intention,
even if it also comes from the intention. When it is
so, it is obvious that intention is superior to the act;
for the intention itself is in the heart itself whilst
the act will flow from another place to the heart. If
(the act) does (this), it is useful; but if it does not,
and it is done heedlessly, it is futile. The intention
without the act is this, that it not be futile. This is
just as if there were a pain in the stomach. When
one takes medicine and it reaches (the belly), the
object is attained. If one smears it on the chest so
that its effect reaches it, it is also beneficial; but it
would be better if it reached the stomach directly.
The object of that ointment which touches the chest
is not the chest but the stomach. It will necessarily
be futile if it does not spread to the stomach. That
which reaches the stomach, even though it does not
reach the chest, will not be futile. . . .[70]

One is to constantly repeat "God! God!" (*al-Lah
al-Lah*), with the heart, not with the tongue.
Indeed, one should not (even) say it with the heart,
for this uttering is like talking to oneself. Rather,
one must be continually in a state of witnessing so
as never to be inattentive. However, this is very
impracticable and difficult: not everyone has the
strength for this, that one's heart have a single
quality and a single state, for people become bored
with doing this. For this reason many different private devotions have been posited. Some have a fixed
form, such as formal prayer, and some are oral such
as reciting/reading the Quran and the glorification;
others are with the heart such as meditation and
reflection lest one become bored. So, at each
moment there is something different to do and in
the change from one state to another there is a rest.
. . . [71]

Know that God Most High has a mystery in the human heart. It is hidden in it just as fire in iron; when a stone is struck on iron the mystery (fire) is made manifest and plain. In the same way listening to fine music (*sama-i khush*) and rhythmic song (*awaz-i mawzun*) excites that essence in the heart. Something appears in it without a person's having any choice about it. The reason for this is the relationship that the essence of every human being has with the World of the Sublime: that which is called the world of spirits. The Sublime World is the world of excellence and beauty; the basis of excellence and beauty is proportion; whatever is in proportion gives proof of the beauty of that world. For, every beauty, excellence, and proportionality that is perceived in this world is all the fruit of the beauty, excellence and proportionality of that world.

Therefore, a sweet, rhythmic, proportioned song also has a resemblance to the marvels of that world. Because of this, an awareness is awakened in the heart. A movement, a yearning or longing is born that the (listener) himself may not understand what it is. This is in a heart which is simple and devoid of being affected by passion and yearning. However, if it is not empty and is occupied with something, that with which it is occupied starts to move and brighten as does a flame when it is breathed upon.

For the person whose heart has been conquered by the fire of the love of God Most High, music is important, for it makes that fire burn hotter. However, for anyone whose heart harbors love for the false, music is fatal poison for him and is forbidden to him.[72]

EPILOGUE

Al-Ghazzali died on Monday the 14th of Jumada Thani AH 505 (December 18, 1111), at the age of fifty-three. Margaret Smith in *Al-Ghazzali the Mystic* relates what took place on the days after his death according to his brother Ahmad.

At dawn of the day of his death, al-Ghazzali performed his ablutions and prayed and then said to his brother, "Bring me my shroud." and taking it, he kissed it and laid it over his eyes and said, "Most gladly do I enter into the Presence of the King," and he stretched out his feet and went forth to meet Him, and so passed into the Paradise of God, "worthy of all honor, of loftier station than the stars, giving more guidance to men than the full moon when darkness has fallen." He was buried outside Tus in a grave near that of the poet Firdousi. Ibn al-Samani records that he visited al-Ghazzali's grave there.

There is a story to the effect that when al-Ghazzali fell ill and felt that his death was approaching, he sent away those who were with him. No one entered his presence until the next morning when they went in as he had bidden them. They found him facing the *qiblah*, clad in his shroud, dead, and at his head they found a sheet of paper bearing these verses:

Say to my friends when they look upon me dead
Weeping for me and mourning me in sorrow
Do not believe that this corpse you see is myself.
In the Name of God I tell you it is not I
I am a spirit and this is nothing but flesh
It was my abode and my garment for a time.

I am a treasure, by a talisman kept hid,
Fashioned of dust which served me as a shrine.
I am a pearl which has left its shell deserted
It was my prison where I spent my time in grief.
I am a bird and this body was my cage
Whence I have now flown forth and it is left as a token,
Praise be to God Who has now set me free
And prepared for me my place in the highest of the heavens.
Now I live in truth with the grave-clothes discarded.
Today I hold converse with the saints above.
Now with no veil between I see God face to face
I look upon the Tablet (*lawh al-mahfuz*) and therein I read
Whatever was and is and all that is to be.
Let my house fall in ruins. Lay my cage in the ground.
Cast away the talisman. It is a token, no more.
Lay aside my cloak. It was but my outer garment.
Place them all in the grave. Let them be forgotten.
I have passed on my way and you are left behind.
Your place of abode was no dwelling-place for me.
Think not that death is death. Nay, it is life,
A life that surpasses all we could dream of here.
While in this world we are granted sleep.
Death is but sleep, a sleep that shall be prolonged.
Be not afraid when death draws near.
It is but the departure for this blessed home.
Think of the mercy and love of your Lord.
Give thanks for His Grace and come without fear.
What I am now even so shall you be
For I know that you are even as I am.
The souls of all people come forth from God.
The bodies of all are compounded alike.
Good and evil alike it was ours.
I give you now a message of good cheer.
May God's peace and joy for evermore be yours.

There were many elegies composed in honor of
al-Ghazzali after his death. The most famous was

that of the poet Abu'l-Muzaffer al-Abiwardi (Ob. 507/1113). Imam Ismail al-Hakimi also express his grief in lines taken from one of the most celebrated qasidas of Abu Tammam:

I wondered how to endure it when deprived of him by death.
I who shed tears of blood when he was away from me.
But these are times when so much seems strange
That we have ceased to wonder thereat.

One of al-Ghazzali's pupils, the well-known Sufi Abu'l Abbas al-Alishi composed verses in praise of both hsi teacher and his teacher's masterpiece, the *Ihya*.

It is related that just after al-Ghazzali's death, Abu'l Abbas Ahmad ibn Abi'l Khayr al-Yamani, known as Sayyad, had a vision. He was sitting at the open gates of heaven and lo, a band of angels were descendign to the earth bearing robes of honor, green in color, and with them a noble steed. They alighted at the head of a certain tomb and brought one forth from his grave. Having invested him with the robes, they set him on that steed and ascended with him to the heavens, continuing to ascend with him from one heaven to another until he had passed through all the seven heavens and ascending beyond them, he traversed the seventy veils. "I was filled with wonder at that," said Abu'l-Abbas, "and I desired to know who that rider was and I was told: 'It is al-Ghazzali,' and I did not know then that he had attained to martyrdom." It is said that al-Ghazzali occupied the position of *qutb*, the supreme head of the mystical hierarchy.

It is also related that someone saw al-Ghazzali after hsi death in a dream and asked about his state. He replied, "If it were not for this strange knowledge, all would be well with us." His biographer is anxious that no one should imagine that this strange knowledge should be interpreted to mean the mystical knowledge of al-Ghazali. This, he holds, would bew a satanic device to prevent others from following in al-Ghazzali's steps and would mean that they were veiled from God and hindered from attaining to the highest degree of sainthood. He interprets the words to mean that since it was a celestial vision of one now in the Presence of God, no longer concerned with the things of sense, the strange knowledge was that which was concerned only with this world, with human affairs and relationships which could have no bearing whatever on life in the world to come, for death means separation from them. So perhaps al-Ghazzali regretted having concerned himself with worldly knowledge which was strange to the heavenly places. But his biographer points out that the knowledge of the mysteries of decotion and what belongs to the world to come could not be strange to one who had attained to that world. Therefore he urges his readers not to misinterpret these words lest they be hindered from seeking spiritual knoweldge, but to acquire worldly knowledge only as much as was really necessary.[73]

NOTES TO THE INTRODUCTION

1 See works like *Timeless Healing: The Power and Biology of Belief* by Herbert Benson; *Why God Won't Go Away: Brain Science and the Biology of Belief* by Andrew Newberg, Eugene D'Aquili and Vince Rause; and *Handbook of Religion and Health* edited by Harold G. Koniz, Michael McCullough and David B. Larsen.

2 Other well known writers and poets born in Tus include Abu Yazid Bistami, Husayn bin Mansur Hallaj, Abu Said Abi'l-Khayr, Nizam al-Mulk, Firdawsi and Umar Khayyam.

3 See Bibliography to the Introduction for the numerous books that detail the life of al-Ghazzali. It is interesting to note that al-Ghazzali wrote the *Alchemy of Happiness* when the First Crusade ruled Jerusalem. Saladin arrived on the scene seventy-seven years after al-Ghazzali's death.

4 See below for the definition of traditional psychology which historically was called the science of ethics or practical wisdom (*hikmat al-amali*).

5 *Knowledge and the Sacred*, p. 68.

6 *Alchemy*, p 841.

7 This is a clear distinction with modern secular psychology which is limited to only treating a human being part by part instead of holistically. See *Alchemy* p 817.

8 *Alchemy*, p 358.

9 *Alchemy,* p 116.

10 *Alchemy*, p 525.

11 *Alchemy*, p 780.

12 *Alchemy*, p 358.

13 *Alchemy*, p 360.

14 *Alchemy*, pp 221-222.

15 *Ibid.*

NOTES TO THE COMMENTARY ON TOPIC ONE OF THE PROLEGOMENA: KNOW YOURSELF

1 *Alchemy*, p 123.

2 *Alchemy*, p 123.

3 *Alchemy*, p 126.

4 *Alchemy*, p 868.

5 *Alchemy*, p 827.

6 *Alchemy*, p 841.

7 The Islamic view of human nature differs from the view of many Christians. Muslims believe that God created the human being complete and perfect and it is the nurturing process that tries to change human nature. Muslims believe that Adam and Eve forgot God's Command and were forgiven by God for their forgetfulness and expelled from Paradise. Many Christians, on the other hand, based on the teachings of Paul (not Jesus) believe that Eve sinned and caused Adam to sin by touching the forbidden fruit. They call this original sin. Because of this original sin, all human beings born from the time of Adam to the time of Jesus lived and died with this original sin. When Jesus died on the cross, Christian theology teaches he saved the human being from that original sin.

8 *Ihya*, IV, 2:2255. Al-Ghazzali defines Divine Grace as "the harmony, agreement, or concord of our will and action with God's Will."

9 See also 3:73, 57:29, 3:272, 3:174, 48:8.

10 *Alchemy*, p. 537.

11 *Alchemy*, pp 841-843.

12 *Alchemy*, pp 907.

13 *Alchemy*, p 918. What al-Ghazzali is saying in this passage is: {that you know the intention" (reason, motivation, purpose) for not doing something that you are able to do but upon reflection do not do so it appears to be out of your control. Intention is a desire or impulse that causes one to act. You act according to your will power. "If you desire to, you do

it; and if you do not desire to, you do not do it." However, when the desire is not in your control (because of your belief system), you may still desire something or not desire something. Moreover, a desire may arise or not arise. The cause of a desire not arising—you are not motivated to do it—is when an erroneous belief system prevents you from doing it. Your motivation or intention is tied to something in this world or the next preventing you from desiring it. A person who does not know these mysteries defers many acts of devotion because there is no motivation to do them.

An example of what al-Ghazzali is referring to here would be: it is the time for formal obligatory prayer. A person believes that God will forgive them his sins or that there is no Hereafter or that missing an obligatory formal prayer is not anything to concern himself about because he knows many Muslims who do not pray, etc. All of these rationalizations according to al-Ghazzali form an erroneous belief system which then does not create the desire in a person to use their power to act and perform the formal obligatory prayer. As a result of not knowing the mysteries of worship one misses many acts of devotion. Their rationalizations prevent their being motivated to perform them.

14 *Alchemy*, p 831.
15 *Alchemy*, p 823.
16 *Alchemy*, pp 515.
17 *Alchemy*, p 556.
18 *Alchemy*, 791.
19 *Alchemy*, 698.
20 *Alchemy*, 824.
21 *Alchemy*, p 527.
22 *Alchemy*, p 527-528.
23 *Alchemy*, p 553.
24 *Alchemy*, p 1010.
25 *Alchemy*, p 832.

26 *Alchemy*, p 1017.
27 *Alchemy*, p 957-958.
28 *Alchemy*, p 931-932.
29 *Alchemy*, p 1034 ff.
30 *Alchemy*, p 1031 ff.
31 *Alchemy*, p 796 ff.
32 *Alchemy*, p 815.
33 *Alchemy*, p 1037.
34 *Alchemy*, p 814.
35 *Alchemy*, p 815.
36 *Alchemy*, p 208.
37 *Alchemy*, p 666.
38 *Alchemy*, p 807.
39 *Alchemy*, p 523.
40 *Alchemy*, p 528.
41 *Alchemy*, p 523.
42 *Alchemy*, p 523.
43 Avicenna, *Canon of Medicine*, pp 32-44. It is important for traditional psychologists to know that Avicenna's Canon of Medicine was translated into Latin not long after it was written. The Latin edition was the major medical textbook for 700 years in Europe.
44 *Ibid*.
45 *Ibid*.
46 *Ibid*.
47 *Ibid*.
48 *Alchemy*, p 515.
49 *Alchemy*, p 513 ff.
50 *Alchemy*, p 517.
51 *Alchemy*, p 516.
52 *Alchemy*, p 515.
53 *Alchemy*, p 517.
54 *Alchemy*, p 518.
55 *Alchemy*, p 535.

56 *Alchemy*, p 535.
57 *Alchemy*, p 526.
58 *Alchemy*, p 905.
59 *Alchemy*, p 906.
60 *Alchemy*, p 508.
61 *Alchemy*, p 913.
62 *Alchemy*, p 536.
63 *Alchemy*, p 909.
64 *Alchemy*, p 525.
65 *Alchemy*, p 667.
66 *Alchemy*, p 909.
67 *Alchemy*, p 525.
68 *Alchemy*, p 526.
69 *Alchemy*, p 909.
70 *Alchemy*, p 910.
71 *Alchemy*, p 234.
72 *Alchemy*, p 425.
73 Al-Ghazzali the Mystic, pp 36-38.

BIBLIOGRAPHY

al-Ghazzali. *Alchemy of Happiness* abridged. Translated by Claud Field. Lahore: Sh. Muhammad Ashraf, 1987. 1100 pages summarized in 60 pages.

al-Ghazzali. *Alchemy of Happiness*. Complete translation by Jay R. Crook. Chicago: Kazi Publications, 2002.

al-Ghazzali. *Confessions*. Translated by Claud Field. Lahore: Sh. Muhammad Ashraf, 1992.

al-Ghazzali. *Deliverance from Error*. Translated by R. J. McCarthy. KY: fons vitae, 1980.

al-Ghazzali. *Faith in Divine Unity and Trust in Divine Providence*. Translated from the *Ihya ulum al-din* (*Kitab al-tawhid wa'l tawakkul*). Translated by David B. Burrell. Cambridge: Islamic Texts Society, 2001.

al-Ghazzali. *Ihya ulum al-din* (*Revival of the Religious Sciences*). Translated by al-Hajj Maulana Fazul ul-Karim. Lahore: Islamic Publications Bureau, n.d.

al-Ghazzali, *Incoherence of the Philosophers*. Translated by Michael E. Marmura. A parallel English-Arabic text. Provo, Utah: Brigham University Press, 1952.

al-Ghazzali. *Inner Dimensions of Islamic Worship*. Translated from the *Ihya ulum al-din*. Leicester; Islamic Foundation, 1990.

al-Ghazzali. *Invocations and Supplications*. Translated from the *Ihya ulum al-din* (*Kitab al-adhkar wal daawat*) by K. Nakamura. Cambridge: Islamic Texts Society, 1996.

al-Ghazzali, *Just Balance* (*al-Qistas al-mustaqim*), Translated by D. P. Brewster. Lahore, Pakistan: Sh. Muhammad

Ashraf, 1987.

al-Ghazzali. *Letters of al-Ghazzali*. Translated by Abdul Qayyum. Lahore: Islamic Publications (Pvt), Ltd. , 1994.

al-Ghazzali. *Mishkat al-anwar*. Translated by W. H. T. Gairdner. Lahore: Sh. Muhammad Ashraf, 1991.

al-Ghazzali. *Mysteries of Almsgiving*. Translated from the *Ihya ulum al-din* (*Kitab asrar al-zakah*) by Nabih Amin Faris. Lahore: Sh. Muhammad Ashraf, 1992.

al-Ghazzali, *Mysteries of Fasting*. Translated from the *Ihya ulum al-din* by Nabih Amin Faris. Lahore: Sh. Muhammad Ashraf, 1992.

al-Ghazzali. *Mysteries of Purity*. Translated from the *Ihya ulum al-din* by Nabih Amir Faris. Lahore: Sh. Muhammad Ashraf, 1991.

al-Ghazzali. *Mysteries of Worship*. Translated from the *Ihya ulum al-din* by Edwin Elliot Calverley. Lahore: Sh. Muhammad Ashraf, 1998.

al-Ghazzali, *Niche of Lights*. Translated by David Buchman. A parallel English-Arabic text. Provo, Utah: Brigham university Press, 1998.

al-Ghazzali. *Ninety-nine Beautiful Names of God* (*al-Maqsad al-asna fi sharh asma Allah al-husna*). Translated by David B. Burrell and Nazih Daher. Cambridge: Islamic Texts Society, 1999.

Al-Ghazzali On Disciplining the Self. Translated from the *Alchemy of Happiness* by Muhammad Nur Abdus Salam (Jay R. Crook). Chicago: Kazi Publications, 2002.

al-Ghazzali. *On Disciplining the Soul and the Two Desires*. Translated from the *Ihya ulum al-din* (*Kitab riyadat al-nafs. Kitab kasr al-shahwatayn)* by T. J. Winter. Cambridge: Islamic Texts Society, 2001.

al-Ghazzali. *On Divine Predicates and their Properties* (*al-Iqtisad fil'itiqad*). Translated by Abdu Rahman Abu Zayd.

India: Kitab Bhavan, 1994.

Al-Ghazzali On Earning a Living and Trade. Translated from *Alchemy of Happiness* by Muhammad Nur (Jay R. Crook). Chicago: Kazi Publications, 2002.

Al-Ghazzali On Enjoining Good and Forbidding Wrong. Translated from *Alchemy of Happiness* by Muhammad Nur Abdus Salam (Jay R. Crook). Chicago: Kazi Publications, 2002.

Al-Ghazzali On Governing and Managing the State. Translated from *Alchemy of Happiness* by Muhammad Nur Abdus Salam (Jay R. Crook). Chicago: Kazi Publications, 2002.

Al-Ghazzali On Hope and Fear. Translated from *Alchemy of Happiness* by Muhammad Nur Abdus Salam (Jay R. Crook). Chicago: Kazi Publications, 2002.

Al-Ghazzali On Journeying. Translated from *Alchemy of Happiness* by Muhammad Nur Abdus Salam (Jay R. Crook). Chicago: Kazi Publications, 2002.

Al-Ghazzali On Knowing This World and the Hereafter. Translated from *Alchemy of Happiness* by Muhammad Nur Abdus Salam (Jay R. Crook). Chicago: Kazi Publications, 2002.

Al-Ghazzali On Knowing Yourself and God. Translated from *Alchemy of Happiness* by Muhammad Nur Abdus Salam (Jay R. Crook). Chicago: Kazi Publications, 2002.

Al-Ghazzali On Listening to Music. Translated from *Alchemy of Happiness* by Muhammad Nur Abdus Salam (Jay R. Crook). Chicago: Kazi Publications, 2002.

Al-Ghazzali On Love, Longing and Contentment. Translated from *Alchemy of Happiness* by Muhammad Nur Abdus Salam (Jay R. Crook). Chicago: Kazi Publications, 2002.

Al-Ghazzali On Marriage. Translated from *Alchemy of Happiness* by Muhammad Nur Abdus Salam (Jay R.

Crook). Chicago: Kazi Publications, 2002.

Al-Ghazzali On Meditation. Translated from *Alchemy of Happiness* by Muhammad Nur Abdus Salam (Jay R. Crook). Chicago: Kazi Publications, 2002.

Al-Ghazzali On Patience and Gratitude. Translated from *Alchemy of Happiness* by Muhammad Nur Abdus Salam (Jay R. Crook). Chicago: Kazi Publications, 2002.

Al-Ghazzali On Reckoning and Guarding. Translated from *Alchemy of Happiness* by Muhammad Nur Abdus Salam (Jay R. Crook). Chicago: Kazi Publications, 2002.

Al-Ghazzali On Remembering Death and the States of the Hereafter. Translated from *Alchemy of Happiness* by Muhammad Nur Abdus Salam (Jay R. Crook). Chicago: Kazi Publications, 2002.

Al-Ghazzali On Repentance. Translated from *Alchemy of Happiness* by Muhammad Nur Abdus Salam (Jay R. Crook). Chicago: Kazi Publications, 2002.

Al-Ghazzali On Spiritual Poverty and Asceticism. Translated from *Alchemy of Happiness* by Muhammad Nur Abdus Salam (Jay R. Crook). Chicago: Kazi Publications, 2002.

Al-Ghazzali On Sufism. Translated from *Alchemy of Happiness* by Muhammad Nur Abdus Salam (Jay R. Crook). Chicago: Kazi Publications, 2002.

Al-Ghazzali On the Duties of Brotherhood. Translated from *Alchemy of Happiness* by Muhammad Nur Abdus Salam (Jay R. Crook). Chicago: Kazi Publications, 2002.

Al-Ghazzali On the Etiquette of Eating. Translated from *Alchemy of Happiness* by Muhammad Nur Abdus Salam (Jay R. Crook). Chicago: Kazi Publications, 2002.

al-Ghazzali. *On the Foundations of the Articles of Faith.* Translated from the *Ihya ulum al-din* (*Kitab qawaid al-aqaid*) by Nabih Amir Faris. Lahore: Sh. Muhammad Ashraf, 1999.

Al-Ghazzali On the Lawful, the Unlawful and the Doubtful.
Translated from *Alchemy of Happiness* by Muhammad
Nur Abdus Salam (Jay R. Crook). Chicago: Kazi
Publications, 2002.

al-Ghazzali. *On the Manners Relating to Eating.* Translated
from the *Ihya ulum al-din* (*Kitab adab al-akl*) by D.
Johnson-Davies. Cambridge: Islamic Texts Society, 2000.

Al-Ghazzali On the Mysteries of the Pillars of Islam.
Translated from *Alchemy of Happiness* by Muhammad
Nur Abdus Salam (Jay R. Crook). Chicago: Kazi
Publications, 2002.

Al-Ghazzali On the Treatment of Anger, Hatred and Envy.
Translated from *Alchemy of Happiness* by Muhammad
Nur Abdus Salam (Jay R. Crook). Chicago: Kazi
Publications, 2002.

Al-Ghazzali On the Treatment of Hypocrisy. Translated from
Alchemy of Happiness by Muhammad Nur Abdus Salam
(Jay R. Crook). Chicago: Kazi Publications, 2002.

*Al-Ghazzali On the Treatment of Ignorance Arising from
Heedlessness, Error and Delusion.* Translated from
Alchemy of Happiness by Muhammad Nur Abdus Salam
(Jay R. Crook). Chicago: Kazi Publications, 2002.

Al-Ghazzali On the Treatment of Love for This World.
Translated from *Alchemy of Happiness* by Muhammad
Nur Abdus Salam (Jay R. Crook). Chicago: Kazi
Publications, 2002.

Al-Ghazzali On the Treatment of Love of Power and Control.
Translated from *Alchemy of Happiness* by Muhammad
Nur Abdus Salam (Jay R. Crook). Chicago: Kazi
Publications, 2002.

Al-Ghazzali On the Treatment of Miserliness and Greed.
Translated from *Alchemy of Happiness* by Muhammad
Nur Abdus Salam (Jay R. Crook). Chicago: Kazi

Publications, 2002.

Al-Ghazzali On the Treatment of Pride and Conceit. Translated from *Alchemy of Happiness* by Muhammad Nur Abdus Salam (Jay R. Crook). Chicago: Kazi Publications, 2002.

Al-Ghazzali On the Treatment of the Harms of the Tongue. Translated from *Alchemy of Happiness* by Muhammad Nur Abdus Salam (Jay R. Crook). Chicago: Kazi Publications, 2002.

Al-Ghazzali On the Treatment of the Lust of the Stomach and the Sexual Organs. Translated from *Alchemy of Happiness* by Muhammad Nur Abdus Salam (Jay R. Crook). Chicago: Kazi Publications, 2002.

Al-Ghazzali On Trust and the Unity of God. Translated from *Alchemy of Happiness* by Muhammad Nur Abdus Salam (Jay R. Crook). Chicago: Kazi Publications, 2002.

Al-Ghazzali On Truthfulness and Sincerity. Translated from *Alchemy of Happiness* by Muhammad Nur Abdus Salam (Jay R. Crook). Chicago: Kazi Publications, 2002.

al-Ghazzali. *Path to Sufism.* Translated by R. J. McCarthy. KY: fons vitae, 2001.

al-Ghazzali. *Some Moral and Religious Teachings.* Translated by Syed Nawab Ali. Lahore: Sh. Muhammad Ashraf, 1995.

al-Ghazzali. *Remembrance of Death and the Afterlife.* Translated from the *Ihya ulum al-din* (*Kitab dhikr al-mawt wa-ma-badahun*) by T. J. Winter. Cambridge: Islamic Texts Society, 1999.

al-Ghazzali. *The Duties of Brotherhood.* Translated from the *Ihya ulum al-din.* Leicester: Islamic Foundation, 1990.

al-Ghazzali. *The Mystic.* Margaret Smith. Chicago: Kazi Publications, 2002.

Avicenna. *The Canon of Medicine.* Chicago: Kazi Publications, 1999.

Benson, Herbert. *Timeless Healing: The Power and Biology of*

Belief. NY: Simon and Schuster, 1996.
Ethical Philosophy of al-Ghazzali. Muhammad Umar ud-Din. Lahore: Sh. Muhammad Ashraf, 1991.
Faith and Practice of al-Ghazzali. W. Montgomery Watt. Edinburgh: Edinburgh University Press, 1952. An abridged translation of *Munqidh min ad-dalal* (Deliverance from Error) and the Beginning of Guidance (*Bidayat al-hidayah*).
Fakhry, Majid. *Al-Ghazzali's Theory of Virtue.* NY: SUNY, 1985.
Koniz, Harold G., Michael McCullough and David B. Larsen. *Handbook of Religion and Health.* NY: Oxford University Press, 2001.
Newberg, Andrew, Eugene D'Aquili and Vince Rause. *Why God Won't Go Away: Brain Science and the Biology of Belief.* NY: Ballantine Books, 2002.